CW00550077

Status Quo
in the 1980s

Greg Harper

sonicbondpublishing.com

Sonicbond Publishing Limited
www.sonicbondpublishing.co.uk
Email: info@sonicbondpublishing.co.uk

First Published in the United Kingdom 2022
First Published in the United States 2022

British Library Cataloguing in Publication Data:
A Catalogue record for this book is available from the British Library

Copyright Greg Harper 2022

ISBN 978-1-78952-244-0

Typeset in ITC Garamond & ITC Avant Garde
Printed and bound in England

Graphic design and typesetting: Full Moon Media

Acknowledgements

Several people have contributed immeasurably to this tome and it would not have been possible to do it without them.

Thanks to Francis Rossi OBE, who took an incredible amount of time out of his Monday afternoon to speak to me and drop several nuggets of largely unknown lore into the publication – a genuine dream come true for me as a professional musician and fan of the band. For a man who wasn't known to be sober through much of the period we discussed, he remembered a staggering amount of particularly small details that could have been lost forever. It may be his expertise at handling 'journos', but he made this first-time author feel not only immediately comfortable but weirdly, like his equal; which I definitely am not. Further, thanks to Lyane Ngan for making it happen. Thanks to John 'Rhino' Edwards for his exquisitely erudite ramblings and his generosity with his time when answering my nerdy questions, both bass-related and Quo-related. He chased up several answers for bits he couldn't remember and called back multiple times to check in on the project. He's a true gentleman and has nothing but positive things to say about his predecessor – unfortunately, sometimes to the detriment of hiding his own ferocious musicianship. Thanks to John Coghlan – a humble man of few but very useful words who used a sunny afternoon to chat to me indoors on the phone. Thanks also to his wife Gillie for setting the meeting up and for being so easy to work with. We discussed the possibility of a remastered CD release of *Organised Crime* and they both seemed interested. I hope it comes off!

Thanks to Pip Williams, who gladly supplied (through John 'Rhino' Edwards) the name of Dick Morrissey as the sax player on 'The Wanderer' but was unable to be interviewed for the project due to a thankfully temporary but unfortunately potent illness just before publication – I'll get him for the next one as he was quite disappointed that he was unable to share his stories here. Thanks to Jeff Rich, who managed to fit me into his busy teaching schedule to share his memories of Quo from behind the drum kit – featuring several tidbits of firework and flatulence-related humour from the band's tour bus hijinks. Thanks to the inimitable, humble and zany Andrew Bown, who corresponded via e-mail while on his holiday and gave his answers to my inane questions in the most amusing and Bown-like way imaginable. His contribution to the band must be buried by the fanbase no more – it should be celebrated and revered as it deserves.

Thanks to Rick Parfitt and Alan Lancaster (who I believe would also have contributed a great deal had they been around to do so) for their contributions to the music I've written about here. Thanks to Jason Hodgson, who is arguably the authority on Quo's recorded (but not always released) output and his bootleg live recordings and studio rarities have come in very handy. Thanks to Thommy Franck whose database of Quo's live career has been immeasurably helpful in writing this book. Thanks to Stephen Lambe at SonicBond for his love of music-related non-fiction and for funding and suggesting the idea for this project. 'Quoincidence', 'cammy' and 'mortified' also deserve an honourable mention for answering a number of my obscure questions. Thanks lads!

Thanks also to Anthony Bentley, musician of his own exceptional ability, Quo partner-in-crime since high school and supportive proofreader and proposer of edits. Thanks to Brian and Hugh – the gold standard of supportive uncles, and thanks to Jeanie and Albie who would have been immensely proud of this little book of trivia. Huge love and thanks to mum, Brad, Lauren, Evelyn and Julia, because you're the best family anyone could have and you believe in my niche passions for decades-old music, records and nerdy trivia but more importantly, in me. Massive love and thanks to Abigail for keeping me on top of my word count, taking my dictation when I got tired of screens (or was driving!) and for being the best partner, anyone could wish for. She's been the true driving force behind getting this book into the hands of fans and without her, I'd have taken all of this useless knowledge to my grave – everyone needs an Abby.

Finally, and most dowdily, thank you to you, the reader. Whether you're a dedicated Quo nut or casual fan (or neither), thank you for taking the time to read this work that took a surprisingly long period of time to write. I hope that whichever category you fall into, you've learned something new or at least seen new value in Quo's most heavily and unfairly criticised recorded pieces of art.

Gregory Harper
April 2022

DECADES | Status Quo in the 1980s

Contents

Introduction 6

Prologue 8

1980: Just Supposin' 13

1981: Never Too Late 22

1982: 1+9+8+2 32

1983: Back to Back 42

1984: The End of the Road 53

1985: Live Aid and Lawsuits 69

1986: In the Army Now... 78

1987: The Sun City Debacle... 93

1988: Ain't Complaining... 97

1989: Perfect Remedy.. 111

Epilogue 123

Introduction

How does one approach writing a book about the mighty Status Quo? Countless have been written before – some by the band themselves. The focus of almost all writing on this formidable ensemble has been focused on the 1970s – their defining decade. But for me, Quo's work in the 1980s shows a group of musicians already at the top of their game, and not quite knowing what to do with their success. Strangely, the period rarely gets more than a glancing mention in the grand scheme of things – the same way the Beatles' *Magical Mystery Tour* record does. These years are underrepresented and vastly undetailed in comparison. Also, writing a book about Status Quo in the 1980s could be considered by some of the remaining fanbase to be sacrilegious or, worse, pointless. After all, where did the hits go? Didn't the band become a parody of itself? Didn't they lose thousands of fans in the process?

The answer is a resounding 'no' to all of these questions. In fact, the band still had several chart-busting hits almost all through the decade, made some of their most artistically adventurous records to date and gained as many fans as they lost. Quo have never pretended to be 'trend setters'. If anything, they were part of their own small European denim-clad counterculture in the '70s, and while the '80s saw the band trying (to a certain extent) to keep up with modern production techniques and radio-friendly musical styles, their musical D.N.A. remained largely unchanged; even with changes in personnel and style drastically affecting the surface sound and visuals of the outfit. Quo were trying to keep afloat creatively, commercially and financially and this resulted in some cosmetic changes in the way the group looked and sounded, but it kept the band alive through what could truly have been the end of the road for the London rockers.

And so I raise a case for the defence. This book seeks to explore the music of Status Quo's turbulent '80s period and examine a decade of great but forgotten creativity with a new perspective and admiration. Hopefully honest and factual but with a smattering of optimism and an unprejudiced viewpoint. Appraising this work has been a joy and listening to these tracks with open ears and an open mind has confirmed what I always believed about every past and present member of Status Quo; they're inimitable, they're prolific, they're versatile and they're a band of real musicians and creatives who can't be accused of not trying to make great sounding records – whether you like the finished product or not. Quo's early periods have been written about countless times, often to the neglect or snubbing of their '80s output. This book aims to address this balance. Although I consider this era of Quo to be my strong suit, researching this book and interviewing members of the band and their creative team has left me more respectful of this ensemble than I ever have been. As the records made during this period are pejoratively held in lower esteem than the hits of the 1970s, learning about them is much more of a challenge due to a comparative lack of readily available information and source material.

Any direct quotes that are not accurately referenced or attributed were given to me through personal correspondence with the speaker in question. Interviews were conducted by the author with John 'Rhino' Edwards, Francis Rossi, Jeff Rich, Andrew Bown and John Coghlan during 2021-2022. Although my publisher and several friends and family proofread this manuscript before publication, any omissions, factual errors, spelling or grammar issues are entirely my own and I'll be happy to fix them in any future editions.

Prologue

Status Quo's illustrious career can be loosely divided up into several different periods. The first of these being the hippy, trippy far-out years of 'Pictures of Matchstick Men' and frilly shirts starting around 1967 and ending in 1970. 1970 to 1972 was the grungy, underground, heads-down boogie years which saw the band totally reinvented as a hard rock and blues outfit – a couple of hit singles but no real hit albums to speak of, but releases from this period are well loved by the hard-core fans. This period served to expand the fanbase and slowly build Quo's reputation for live performance. Third, we get the glory years – 1972-1979 – a period of number one albums, a number one single and a reputation on a global level, but to shrink the career of such a British institution down to a singular chapter seems inconsiderate; but down to a single paragraph, unforgivably churlish.

Formed in 1962 at Sedgehill Comprehensive School in Lewisham, 'The Scorpions' previously known for a few weeks as 'The Paladins' were a band made up of Francis Rossi on guitar and vocals, Alan Lancaster on bass guitar and vocals, Jess Jaworski on keyboards and Alan Key on drums. Rossi, Lancaster and Key had met in the school orchestra before deciding to form their own group.

In 1963, a chance encounter with air cadet drummer John Coghlan had him replacing Key after Rossi and Lancaster were taken with his technique on a snare drum. The band soon changed their name to 'The Spectres'. After a small number of local appearances, they were approached by local gas fitter Pat Barlow who offered to manage the band. The boys left school in 1965 and with that, Jaworski decided to also leave the group and was promptly replaced by organist Roy Lynes.

Another chance encounter was to be the most important in the history of the band. Guitarist and vocalist Rick Parfitt was playing with a trio called The Highlights at a summer season at Butlins and came in to listen to the Spectres who were also working at the Minehead resort at the time. Parfitt and Rossi became the best of friends during their time together and promised to work with each other after the season was over in one capacity or another.

Now writing original material and scoring a recording contract in 1966, the band rebranded for a short while as 'Traffic' but soon changed it again to Traffic Jam to prevent any confusion with Steve Winwood's band at the time. A handful of singles were released as both The Spectres and Traffic/Traffic Jam but to no commercial success.

By 1967, manager Barlow insisted on recruiting Parfitt to the band to provide another lead voice to balance the ensemble out and, soon after, the group changed their name to 'The Status Quo' after liking the sound of the name but not really caring about its meaning.

The Status Quo's breakout hit came in the form of 'Pictures of Matchstick Men' – a piece of pure psychedelia scoring the band a number seven hit on the UK singles charts. After the follow-up 'Black Veils of Melancholy' reached only number 51, a Ronnie Scott and Marty Wilde-penned tune called 'Ice in the Sun' gave the band another hit at number eight but soon, the success dried up and wouldn't come back around for two years.

Becoming fed up with chasing the fashionable sounds and images of the fickle psychedelia scene, the band began to embrace their own newly evolving musical tastes for blues-inflected boogie music. Ditching their flower-power image, the band rebels against their previous success to reinvent themselves as 'Status Quo' – a hard rock and blues outfit. Through arduous touring and relearning how to make records that sounded how they wanted them to sound, Quo built up a new following – of long-haired, denim-toting rockers and students; eager for the laid-back grooves of 'Umleitung' and the frantic shuffles of 'Gotta Go Home'. Organist Lynes eventually left the band after falling in love on the road and his slightly older age was already instilling in him a desire to settle down with a steadier income.

Chart success for albums was a slow burner, but early singles in their new bluesy style like 'Down the Dustpipe' and 'In My Chair' hit number 12 and number 21, respectively, in 1970. Quo's first studio album to break into the top 40 was 1972's *Piledriver* and from there, Quo became an 'albums band' and as a result, singles also began selling in their hundreds of thousands. Although now working quite well as a quartet that would eventually become known as the 'Frantic Four' by fans, Rossi was insistent on using keyboards on some studio recordings and so Andrew Bown was drafted in during the *Hello!* album to contribute some piano to 'Blue Eyed Lady' and later 'Ease Your Mind' and 'Mad About the Boy' for the 1976 album *Blue For You*. Bown had met the band while working with The Herd and Rossi, Parfitt and Lancaster had struck up a friendship with the multi-instrumentalist, although only Rossi really saw the band as having a permanent space for keyboards. Among The Herd's crew was also Robert 'Bob' Young; he was also soon swiped by Rossi as a songwriting partner, harmonicist to the band and later, as a tour manager.

To all intents and purposes, Quo only had one final mountain to climb by the mid-1970s. They had done almost everything else with their hit records and sell-out tours but Quo had yet to crack America. From the 1972 *Piledriver* album to (most of) *Blue For You* in 1976, Quo had been largely producing their own records and had been doing a very good job of it too. Quo's management felt that American audiences had a more refined taste for pop production and began insisting on the band using outside but experienced producers to not only help the band make records but teach them the most up-to-date techniques for them to make their own.

Enter Pip Williams, a guitarist, producer and arranger of fine pedigree, having worked with Mud, The Walker Brothers, Catherine Howe and Graham Bonnet, among others. Brought in by Quo's then label Vertigo, and the band's manager (Colin Johnson) to break away from their successful and established but raw and unrefined sound, Pip's only mission was to make Quo's brand of rock palatable for the conservative American taste. Pip specialised in multi-tracking guitars, pristine vocal capture and arranging & overdubbing instruments that were not native to the Quo brand, such as horn sections and auxiliary percussion. Furthermore, he worked hard to tidy up the overall sound – putting the vocals higher in the mix and recording the basic rhythm tracks with as little microphone 'bleed' as possible. The first resulting album was *Rockin' All Over the World* in 1977.

The album was a huge turning point for Quo – the title track (perhaps Quo's best known although penned by CCR's John Fogerty) was released as a single and reached number three in the UK singles chart. The album itself peaked at number five on the UK album chart and many of the tracks found their way into Quo's live sets ever since.

Although much more polished than previous efforts, the record also suffered from a lack of 'bottom end' (bass frequencies), meaning many fans were confused and disappointed by Quo's new sound. The lack of 'thump' from the record may be down to the fact that the record was mixed down on a pair of Auratone speakers – small cones that emulated the sound of American AM radios at the time. Despite the domestic and European success, the Americans still were not taking the bait. Williams thinks this may be due to Quo's reluctance to build their reputation from scratch through arduous touring at the bottom of the bill in the States, but this is pure conjecture on the producer's part.

Pip produced Quo's next album, *If You Can't Stand the Heat…* released in 1978 and hitting number three on the UK album chart.

Unfortunately, there were still no USA hits to speak of. The album featured the David Katz Horns (most notably on 'Let Me Fly') and female backing vocalists Stevie Lange, Joy Yates and Jackie Sullivan – a first for the band.

In a last-ditch effort to secure a US hit, the 1979 *Whatever You Want* album was released with two different mixes. The original Pip Williams mix made it to number four on the UK chart, while the Steve Klein mix was released as *Now Hear This* in 1980 in the USA but did not trouble the Billboard chart in any meaningful way. Williams seemed to have suppressed his passion for auxiliary arranging here as the album went back to Quo's guitar-heavy sound, albeit more restrained with considered lead guitar breaks.

Then, things inevitably begin to change. Frictions in the band emerge and decisions become harder to make as the democratic strands unravel. The 1980s saw all of this and more for Status Quo. Perhaps more than any other decade, the band saw the highest peaks and the lowest troughs in both their professional and personal lives. With the decade coming to a close, Quo were still riding high in Europe but were becoming increasingly frustrated with the lack of traction across the pond. Their management would soon begin to throw the kitchen sink at trying to break America from afar, with the band growing increasingly ambivalent towards building a following there.

With Williams having taught the band a little about production over the last three albums, they were to set out on their own to keep costs down and now retain complete control over their sound. Williams spent the next couple of years working with the likes of The Sweet, Kiki Dee, the Moody Blues, glamour model duo Blonde on Blonde and The Sweet's Brian Connolly; leaving Status Quo largely to their own devices for the time being.

And so Status Quo entered the 1980s with eight UK top 5 albums and 18 UK top 40 singles under their belt. By this point in their career, they had secured themselves a reputation for being a formidable live act with successful hit records to boot. Singles like 'Paper Plane' (number eight – 1972), 'Caroline' (number five – 1973), and 'Down Down' (number one – 1974) had led the way to more polished productions like 'Rockin' All Over the World' (number three – 1977) and 'Whatever You Want' (number four – 1979). So Quo, despite being hounded by the press for no reason other than for using a harmonic vocabulary akin to the three chords of Chuck Berry, The Beatles and Elvis Presley; were a household name with a loyal, record-buying, gig-attending fanbase that would ride the wild rollercoaster of the 1980s – a period of great change, heartbreak, failures and successes.

1980: Just Supposin'

Just Supposin'

Personnel:

Francis Rossi: guitar, vocals

Rick Parfitt: guitar, vocals

Alan Lancaster: bass guitar, vocals

John Coghlan: drums

Additional Musicians:

Andy Bown: keyboards

Bernie Frost: backing vocals

Bob Young: harmonica

Produced by John Eden, Status Quo

Record Label: Vertigo

Recorded: Windmill Lane Studio, Dublin, 1980

Release date: 17 October 1980

Highest UK chart place: 4

Running time: 40:41

Side one: 'What You're Proposing' (Francis Rossi, Bernie Frost) – 4:18, 'Run to Mummy' (Rossi, Andy Bown) – 3:12, 'Don't Drive My Car' (Rick Parfitt, Bown) – 4:32, 'Lies' (Rossi, Frost) – 3:56, 'Over the Edge' (Alan Lancaster, Keith Lamb) – 4:33

Side two: 'The Wild Ones' (Lancaster) – 4:02, 'Name of the Game' (Rossi, Lancaster, Bown) – 4:29, 'Coming and Going' (Parfitt, Bob Young) – 6:21, 'Rock 'n' Roll' (Rossi, Frost) – 5:23

The band arrived at Windmill Lane Studios in Dublin during February 1980 – a studio equipped with a then state-of-the-art MCI JH 500 mixing desk and JH24 tape machine. The band had decided to self-produce the album alongside friend and producer John Eden, who had worked on the last three albums as an engineer under Pip Williams. Eden was a prolific engineer but had little producing experience at the time, but would later go on to produce Graham Bonnet, The Climax Blues Band and Andy Fraser of Free.

Francis Rossi:

[Having a producer on board] would appease everyone in the band. I would say, 'I'm not taking it on!' [I didn't want to] fight anybody… but I could talk through the producer. My will went through the producer or the engineer.

In the months leading up to the sessions, Eden had helped Rick and Francis build their own recording facilities at home and Lancaster was fully equipped in the same fashion in Australia where he was now living. This meant that the writing and arranging of the songs was done before the studio sessions at Windmill Lane and the standard of the demo recordings for everyone's contributions were of higher quality than usual. This in turn meant that the studio time could be spent on recording rather than teaching each other the songs and discussing how a particular section should go. Any compositional changes were made in the evenings back at the Jurys Hotel where the band and Eden were staying.

John Eden, posted to the *SQMB*, on 1 October 2008:

> It was our second visit to record in Dublin – four years earlier, we had attempted what became *Rockin' All Over the World,* but the studio just didn't work out. In the time that had elapsed from *Rockin' All Over the World*, *If You Can't Stand the Heat*, and *Whatever You Want*, a great new studio had emerged called Windmill Lane and it was a very different set-up from the other studio we had visited years earlier… Francis had been spending quite a bit of time in Ireland writing with Bernie. Richard had been in the Channel Islands and Ireland, both of which were temporary living areas for tax reasons. Alan, I believe, had made Australia his permanent home. John was based in the Isle of Man, which was no more than an hour's flight to Heathrow and Andy, I think, was living in Barnes. So in respect of four of the band members, it was a nearby location out of England to [their] main residences. My letter of agreement at the time was to record tracks for two albums.

Unfortunately, the recording was temporarily halted due to Parfitt falling sick with a virus and beginning to suffer from back pain.

During another session in a different room at Windmill Lane in May 1980, the band set out to continue recording two albums' worth of material. Quo had used the first session to complete all the instrumental backing, vocals and basic mixing for what would become the *Just Supposin'* album and this latest session would see them record the basic guide tracks for what would become the *Never Too Late* album. The songs picked for the *Just Supposin'* release were fresh and showed the band dipping their collective toe back into the water of commercialism after the rockier *Whatever You Want* album. The album reached number four in the UK album chart and spawned three hit singles. All of the left-over tracks from both sessions would later be used for the *Never Too Late* album appearing in the UK album chart five months later.

Just Supposin' is notable for being the first album to feature Francis' co-writer Bernard Frost in such a prolific capacity – but Bernard Frost was not new to the group by any means. 'Bernie' first met the band at one of Quo's many regular appearances at the Greyhound pub in Croydon on New Year's Eve 1971. His first appearance as a writer on a Quo release was with Alan Lancaster on the *Piledriver* album of 1972. This unexpected pairing provided the ballad 'A Year' – an album track that features a theme of bereavement and Beatle-esque vocal harmonies. Rossi had then produced Frost's second single, 'The House', which featured a backing band of Quo's Frantic Four, with Lancaster's role being deputised by Andy Pyle of the Kinks and John Sinclair of Uriah Heep on keyboards. Frost became a regular writer with Rossi in the late '70s and stayed in the Quo camp until around 2000, after he experienced financial issues and severed all ties with Rossi and the band. He sadly passed away in 2019 from lymphoma.

'What You're Proposin'' was not just the lead single for the album but was the first track on it. The opening riff was inspired by an argument with a local guitar dealer that had tried one-too-many times to rip Francis off, although the bright, jolly, major-key statement contrasts with the drama of the origin story. The record features Rossi and co-writer Bernie Frost in a natural-sounding two-part harmony throughout. It was a big hit for the band peaking at number two in the UK and has been a regular part of the set since its release. The song's verses and choruses are built around just two chords, but the multitrack layering of guitars and the tightness of the band on this fast-paced rock number is not to be underestimated – even more impressive that it was recorded without a click track.

John Coghlan:

I don't ever remember using click tracks at all in those days. I was a drummer who kept good time so we never did. Me, Al, and Rick were the rhythm section and we would tape those basic rhythm tracks live at the same time – often with Francis, too when he wasn't behind the mixing desk. We rehearsed well and worked well together – if you've got a good rhythm section, you've got a good band. I remember the first time I heard that [demo]. Francis played drums on it at his home studio and [for the finished studio version] I more or less copied exactly what

Francis played. I would occasionally give my advice on certain songs, but things were always kicked about in rehearsals first – that's how we learned the songs. I'm proud of that track in particular – the drumming is quite busy (for a Quo song); I thought it was a very good song.

A twin harmony guitar solo appears around 2:10 with a cheeky change of key and shows Rossi's talent for composing lead breaks. The single was backed with an instrumental blues jam titled 'AB Blues' – as the take was collectively improvised, the royalties for composition would be split equally.

John Eden, posted to the *SQMB* on 10 August 2008:

> I recall several reasons this came about. Seemed like a good idea to have the band jam and see what came up. It did not use up an album track and offered the fans a track that wasn't on the vinyl album (although I realise it became part of the CD reissue later on). It solved any issue about who had the B-side writer/publisher split as everyone had equal credit.

It has some overdubs over the final portion of the track as Rossi harmonises his own guitar solo. This track seems as though John Eden only just managed to hit record as the band started up the jam session, as you can hear the tape machine zip into action in the opening second of the cut. This track was more than likely recorded at Parfitt's home studio.

'Run to Mummy' has Bown's compositional fingerprints all over it. The opening riff is straight out of his playbook, as is the lyrical content – a toxic relationship that neither party really wants to leave. His high backing vocals are quite loud in the mix and he clearly directed the arrangement for his own composition. Lancaster's bass line drives the track consistently and melodically, aiding and abetting Coghlan's rudimentary but massive-sounding groove and even throwing in some of his trademark slides as the fade-out begins.

'Don't Drive My Car' is a Bown/Parfitt composition that was released as a double A-side single with 'Lies'. While the lyrical content is quite on the nose, the arrangement builds nicely to a rip-roaring solo from Rossi around 2:13. The song opens with Parfitt's swamp-rock, drop D riff quickly accompanied by John Coghlan's cowbell groove and Bown's whistling organ. The song features some tasteful extended chords that are not regular features of Quo songs and there are some especially crunchy chords in the build-up to the solo.

Andrew Bown:

I clearly remember sitting down to write with Richard one day and he just picked up a guitar and virtually played 'Don't Drive My Car' – from nothing. I think my sole contribution was a couple of obnoxious chords as an instrumental. As for writing with Rick, well, we generally started in the pub. Then usually back to his house in the country where he had a billiard room (later to be a kosher recording studio) and we'd sit on the floor with a bottle of Scotch and splash around until something sounded reasonable. Which of course, it would after half a bottle. Wrong. But we had a lot of laughs.

While it has been in the live set on and off for some time, Rossi admitted that the song was 'not one of my faves' but changed his opinion when it was rerecorded in a quasi-manouche style for the 2014 release *Aquostic*.

If 'Don't Drive My Car' screamed Parfitt/Bown, 'Lies' screamed Rossi/ Frost louder – more commercial sounding and more focus on the lyrics and melody than instrumental hooks. Frost can be heard providing falsetto vocal backing in the style of ELO – a favourite band of Rossi's (and the general public) at the time – but it was not a sound Quo fans predicted would be on their turntables. Although expertly recorded, this song seems to signpost the beginning of Rossi's ambivalence towards composed instrumental sections, riffs and solos as if his sole focus is the lyrics and tune. The vocal sound achieved here was captured and curated by Rossi and Eden double-tracking the vocal with an AKG 414 EB microphone.

John Eden posted this to the *SQMB*:

I've worked with some vocalists that were literally too perfect at tracking so that you end up with a phased vocal, others that can never sing the same line twice. Francis, however, just has a gift for the perfect blend… and always produced great-sounding double-tracked vocals when we had fun together in the early 80s. Well, once the magic was captured, I would playback this track in Francis' cans panned half left with his new vocal half right. This helped him differentiate the tracks and place his phrasing against the 1st track. On my monitors, I would pan hard left and right these vocal tracks and analyse all pitch and timing that way. Occasionally we may hit a line that wouldn't work, so we'd go back to the 1st track, fix the problem line or word and then track it. Once complete, pan both back to centre and just ghost the double track a little under the main track and that's it. Sometimes I'd also switch in the varispeed on the tape machine and drop the pitch just a tad for the double track and there were times when I'd do this for the first track as well!

The 'Lies'/'Don't Drive My Car' double A-side single reached a respectable number 11 on the UK singles chart. 'Lies' is an ear worm that has its life force in the production and delivery of the lead vocal.

Bassist Alan Lancaster's first of three compositional contributions to the album came in the form of 'Over the Edge', written with soon-to-be-regular collaborator Keith Lamb of glam rockers Hush. While this medium-paced shuffle rocks along with typical Lancaster aplomb, the falsetto backing vocals make another appearance that, for some listeners, simply don't fit. Rossi takes over some of the vocal refrain at the end – possibly a last-minute overdub. The lyrics aren't likely to win anyone any Grammys, but the song made it into the live set and became something of a fan favourite in concert.

The second side of the album opens with one of Lancaster's best songs to date. 'The Wild Ones' is an allegorical song about being the underdog, the outsider and the misunderstood stranger – a perfect metaphor for not just Status Quo and their fanbase but for Alan as an individual who was beginning to feel out of place in his own group. Written almost like a piece of advice to younger, less experienced upstarts, 'The Wild Ones' is a nostalgic shuffle with a fantastic spread of backing vocals and open string legato licks making up the main riff. There are undertones of 'epicness' about the track until the change of scene at 1:55; a new, bluesier feel that is reminiscent of the Quo of five years earlier. When the verse returns, it arrives with a renewed optimism as the track fades out and the arrangement densifies. In a 2009 interview with Arjen de Graaf, Eden said, '

> Francis, in particular, saw the potential in this song and had a great deal to do with how it turned out. I always felt Francis was/is always interested first and foremost in the best song for S.Q. no matter who wrote it'.

'Name of the Game' is an obscure cut that seems pieced together with different parts – likely from different composers. It's rare that by this point, Lancaster was actively writing 'with' Rossi or Bown purely down to differences in creative process and direction.

Andrew Bown, in *FTMO Magazine*, April 2021:

Co-writing is a difficult thing for me. It can be fabulously rewarding and great fun or it can turn into 'art by committee', which never really works. I usually have an idea that fits with someone else's idea, then away we go, sometimes separately and sometimes together.

The lyrics are leaning into dark territory, which implies the deep thinker Bown was the main lyricist; in this instance, a man accused (perhaps wrongly) of various misdemeanours such as sexual assault and murder.

'Coming and Going' is Parfitt's only other lead vocal on the album and while the song may not be made of much from a technical standpoint, Bob Young's wailing, soulful harmonica playing is given the spotlight almost from the get-go. The song was written at Young's house with Parfitt on guitar, Young on harp, and a primitive drum machine. Drinks had been imbibed and is evident from the cassette recording of the demo that has seen a release on deluxe editions of the album. Parfitt had discovered a penchant for dropped tunings long ago and featured here is a rare one for Quo – drop C tuning. It's the longest cut on the record and gives Young the opportunity to let loose on the rather long fade out.

When fans saw that a track called 'Rock 'n' Roll' would be closing the album, you can imagine their excitement and anticipation for a heavy pièce de résistance of bluesy shuffles, boisterous guitar licks and soulful vocals – but they would be colossally disappointed when the needle reached it. What they got instead was a heartfelt, country-tinged ballad about Rossi's growing ambivalence towards the music business and the hard rock reputation he was expected to uphold. More falsetto vocal backing and up-front synthesiser riffs seem to signal to the listener that Status Quo, as we knew it, is coming to an end. The song was written with Andy Bown, who would later compose 'Rock Til You Drop' with a similarly oxymoronic sound world. Released as a single a year later, the track made it to number eight in the UK chart but not without alienating a few fans in the process. It was played live for a short while and was re-recorded for the *Aquostic* project in 2014. Legend has it that while Rossi was overdubbing the guitar solo alone with producer John Eden late one August evening, the control room telephone rang just as the end of the tape was reached – it was the news that Heidi Parfitt, Rick's two-year-old daughter, had been killed in a disastrous accident at the Parfitt family home after falling into their swimming pool. The guitar solo is one of Rossi's most melodic and emotionally charged and if the story is true, it takes on a visceral sadness and despair that can be felt rather than heard.

Status Quo did not appear for any live dates in 1980 – the first year that they hadn't performed as a band since their formation. Although some mimed promotional appearances took place, the band did not tour their live set. This was due to Parfitt's worsening back problems and so the German tour scheduled for the beginning of the year (and several recording dates) had to be cancelled. A winter tour was also out of the question as Parfitt mourned the loss of his daughter. The 1982 tour programme explained the reasons a little more delicately:

Francis Rossi:

We wanted to prove to ourselves that we could do something different, to make an album and release it without having to tour to back it up. We were so fed up with everyone saying it couldn't be done, that we thought: 'Why not do it now, now we've got the chance'?

Rick Parfitt:

Somehow it didn't seem right to tour in 1980. I had arthritis at the beginning of the year, and there were various other reasons why we chose not to do it. In the end, it was probably the right decision.

Now temporarily a little short of work, Bown took this opportunity to work as the bassist with his friends Pink Floyd on their 31-date *The Wall* tour. This gig would involve Bown and the rest of the musicians in a secondary 'surrogate' band playing characters on stage in various roles and costumes – something Bown would later remember fondly.

Andrew Bown in *FTMO Magazine* in April 2021:

...I enjoyed Pink Floyd's *The Wall* so much. Rapid costume changes. Mask! Next instrument! Get in position! No doubt about it – kept the blood moving. Although having said that, Quo probably gets the blood moving better than anything else. Certainly, a lot faster.

Roussos, Mitchell & Coe

A Quo song released as the closing ballad on 1994's *Thirsty Work* was originally a much older song that Rossi and Frost sold to million-selling Greek singer Demis Roussos for his 1980 album *Man of the World*. 'Sorry', is a slow 4/4 acoustic ballad that bears considerable resemblance to the

structure and delivery of Quo's later re-recording. In R
instruments are provided by the composers and Rossi'
even audible at the beginning of the track. The highli
is the soaring vocal arrangement towards the back en
Unfortunately, when the Roussos version of the track
stand-alone single, it failed to chart.

In one of their more surreal appearances, Rossi and Frost appea
guest vocalists on the Mitchell/Coe Mysteries album *Exiled This* concept
album (in the style of Jeff Wayne's *War of the Worlds*) was conceived by
Fylde coast composers Bob Mitchell and Steve Coe and featured a stellar
cast of studio musicians and production team alongside household
names from the UK music industry. The track featuring Rossi and Frost –
'Ships in the Night' – is about the possibility of extra-terrestrial life and
features more of Frost's quintessential falsetto vocals. The instrumental
track, provided by guitarist Ray Russell, bassist Andy Pask, drummer Paul
Thompson and keyboardists Chris Parren and Dave Lawson, is expertly
played and arranged and features several melodic hooks of its own.
The harmony twists and turns throughout, but the closing section of
increasingly clashy foreign synth chords leave the listener in no doubt
that this is a piece of 'art rock' that is prepared to dip its toe into the
avant-garde in order to depict the arrival of unknown entities. The album
was not a commercial success but makes for interesting listening when
engaging with the project in its entirety.

Never Too Late

ever Too Late

Personnel:
Francis Rossi: guitar, vocals
Rick Parfitt: guitar, vocals
Alan Lancaster: bass guitar
John Coghlan: drums
Additional Musicians:
Andy Bown: keyboards
Bernie Frost: backing vocals
Produced by John Eden, Status Quo
Record Label: Vertigo
Recorded: Windmill Lane Studio, Dublin, 1980
Release date: 13 March 1981
Highest UK chart place: 2
Running time: 38:02
Side one: 'Never Too Late' (Francis Rossi, Bernie Frost) – 3:59, 'Something 'Bout You Baby I Like' (Richard Supa) – 2:51, 'Take Me Away' (Rick Parfitt, Andy Bown) – 4:49, 'Falling in Falling Out' (Parfitt, Bown, Bob Young) – 4:15, 'Carol' (Chuck Berry) – 3:41
Side two: 'Long Ago' (Rossi, Frost) – 3:46, 'Mountain Lady' (Alan Lancaster) – 5:06, 'Don't Stop Me Now' (Lancaster, Bown) – 3:43, 'Enough is Enough' (Rossi, Parfitt, Frost) – 2:54, 'Riverside' (Rossi, Frost) – 5:04

Just five months after the release (and success) of *Just Supposin'*, Vertigo released the remaining tracks from the *Supposin'* sessions on the 1981 album *Never Too Late*. It also featured three additional tracks that had not been recorded in Dublin during these sessions. Collaborator Bob Young had stepped down from tour managing duties in January and was replaced by Iain Jones – fairly new to Quo's management team, Quarry, but known to the band as a keyboard tech for Andy Bown since the *Rockin' All Over the World* tour. To a certain degree, Young also felt usurped by Bernie Frost in the creative pursuits of the band and had begun to take a back seat as a lyricist – especially as a collaborator with Francis Rossi. In an interview with Mick Wall in 2008, Rossi claimed that in hindsight, 'someone' (rumoured but never confirmed to be someone in the upper echelons of the band's management) wanted Young out of the picture so that they could 'rip Status Quo off' – something that would not have been possible if Young was around to look after their business.

The 66-date *Never Too Late* tour was the first in the band's history that didn't feature Bob Young in any capacity and the first to be used to promote two albums simultaneously as no tour had taken place for the previous album due to Parfitt's back problems and personal heartache over the loss of his daughter. The 'Never Too Late 1982 Tour' was plagued with its own issues – mostly around both Rossi and Parfitt fighting throat infections at different times, meaning Lancaster had to cover vocal duties where applicable. The recording of the album had also been temporarily halted due to Parfitt falling asleep with a cigar between his fingers after partying with Thin Lizzy's Scott Gorham resulting in a brief loss of impetus, according to Eden. Parfitt struggled to play for a day or two due to the temporary damage to his hand.

John Eden, posted to the *SQMB*, 1 October 2008:

Fortunately, he was lucky, he healed quickly, but we did lose a bit of momentum in the tracking stage as he could not play and we moved onto overdubs for a few days on tracks we already had in the can.

John Coghlan:

I thought Pip was great and I liked John Eden too. I think a lot of bands like the idea of producing themselves because they know what they want and I think that's how [certain people in Status Quo] wanted it to be. But then, some bands like producers. As for the drumming, I was usually left to it – 'that's good, John' and get on with it. They liked what I did and Francis always gave me credit. I think our [methods] worked really well and we were lucky.

The cover art was designed by Mancunian designer Pat Carroll and it featured another missile (like on the twin album *Just Supposin'*) being halted by a human hand as it headed for Earth. This record remains the only album to date to officially feature Francis Rossi as lead vocalist on every track. Lancaster maintained that this was a 'throw-away' album compiled of the tracks that never made the cut for *Just Supposin'*, but the album spawned not only a hit single but entered the UK album charts at number two.

The album opens with the title track – a four-minute rock number with seemingly idealist advisory overtones regarding the state of the planet and the way humans treat one another. This is almost certainly where the idea for the cover artwork came from. The song begins with a tight semiquaver figure played by the whole band before composer Rossi's lead vocal enters, sitting low in the mix in true Quo style. He's once again harmonised by co-writer Bernie Frost who also provides more falsetto counterpoint to the main vocal during the later verses. The double-tracked solo breaks are a strong addition to the overall production.

The second track (and only single from the album) is a cover of Richard Supa's 'Something 'Bout You Baby I Like' – originally a hit for Tom Jones in 1974. Rossi was rather taken with the hit Rita Coolidge and Glen Campbell had with it in 1980 and decided to give it the Quo treatment. Parfitt is given lead vocals on the bridge sections (just as Coolidge was) of the tune, which colours the arrangement in a highly typical fashion. There's a functional, temperate but well-executed guitar solo that is played with a little more gusto in live scenarios that appears to be directly inspired by Campbell's own solo break. While the track has a typical Quo groove, the fade-out of the song features drum fills 'played in' by Rossi on a drum machine during post-production but Coghlan's drums underneath sound tight and with a crisp, biting snare.

John Coghlan:

Those two albums were all Premier drums – I had a good deal with them at the time. We never swapped snares or cymbals between songs or takes – we used to set them up and leave them.

There's also an overdubbed, phased hi-hat added to the mix too – a post-production decision made by a LinnDrum toting Rossi.

John Eden, posted to the *SQMB*, 1 October 2008:

John played well on the Dublin sessions and was pretty consistent, one or two incidents but no more than I had got used to… he did not write, which if he had may have helped in the feel aspect of interpretation of the songs but maybe not… Francis is a pretty good drummer and keyboard player and certainly had frustrations at times with John's feel for his songs.

This recording is one of few from the *Never Too Late/Just Supposin'* sessions that was not recorded in Dublin and was likely tracked at either the record company studios or Parfitt's home studio. A low-budget-looking video directed by 10cc's Godley & Creme was used for promotion purposes and depicts a fair-haired, denim-clad rocker working on cars, buying records and gearing up for a Quo concert. The single reached a respectable number nine on the UK chart in February 1981 and was added to the live set for the 1981 tour. It's also been a regular feature of the live set since the late 1990s.

'Take Me Away' is a typically quirky Bown composition with help from Parfitt (most probably providing the opening riff). The minor key shuffle is a solid vehicle for Lancaster's pumping root notes and Rossi's simple-but-effective slide playing around the vocals in the choruses. Those licks appear again alongside his solo panned in the left channel. The solo is very overdriven, even for Rossi, who appears to have composed the section with repetition in mind in order to create another hook for the song. The same solo appears again over the fade-out with small variations in the phrasing and composition.

Andrew Bown:

'Take Me Away' was inspired by Rick's dreadful experience stuck at an airport – somewhere in Germany, I think – with polyarthritis and he was in a bad way. In the end, he chartered a plane to get himself home. Wow. Bigtime rock'n'roll! I don't think we actually collaborated on it, although I used the 'B tuning', which definitely started it off.

A three-way writing credit for track four goes to Bown, Parfitt and Bob Young. 'Falling In, Falling Out' is a country-flavoured stomp cut that sees Rossi and Parfitt in a neat trademark harmony throughout, although some possibly deliberate slips into unison at the end of the occasional phrase jump out of the stereo field. Bown eventually adds his own backing vocal to the blend and plays an inverted pedal tone ostinato over the choruses to provide a synthesised string arrangement that builds as the track progresses. Lancaster roots the groove with relatively funky broken octaves and occasionally finds them doubled with a Moog synth. There's an element of reggae here, too – the pre-chorus breaks down into a neat little groove with Coghlan using the opportunity to kick the chorus back up a notch upon entry. There's a pretty guitar solo courtesy of Rossi around the 2:48 mark that is only made up of a few repeated notes but seems to suit the composition distinctively.

The first side closes with a cover of Chuck Berry's 'Carol'. Quo have recorded several other Berry songs over the years ('Bye Bye Johnny', 'Memphis Tennessee', 'You Never Can Tell', 'Rock n Roll Music', 'No Particular Place to Go') and this cut is among the best. Again, recorded somewhere other than Dublin, there is a distinctly different sound to the track. There's a furious solo courtesy of Rossi, who plays effortlessly into the key change that accompanies it. For such a simple song, there's a fairly loud and dense mix that seems to stick this track's head above the parapet. It was played live a handful of times and was dropped from the set after a couple of shows.

Side two opens with 'Long Ago' – a Rossi/Frost composition that, while catchy, isn't a straightforward puzzle to solve lyrically. It's a groovy shuffle number that features subtle time signature changes (to 3/4) and double-tracked lead lines. There's a thunderous bottom-end to the track courtesy of Lancaster, and Parfitt can clearly be heard in the vocal mix with Rossi and Frost in the choruses. The fade-out puts Frost's falsetto vocal talents on show once again. It's highly likely that Rossi wanted this to become a key characteristic of the band's '80s sound.

'Mountain Lady' is a Lancaster composition that is certainly one of the highlights of the whole project. After Lancaster's count-in, his fairly psychedelic lyric is accompanied by a beautifully constructed chord sequence that explores the entire sonic architecture of the key and allows the melody to soar in the bridge section. The opening synth lines may or may not have been Lancaster's idea, but they certainly fly in the face of his apparent distaste towards bringing electronic elements to the band. Interestingly, Rossi has taken lead vocals here. Interesting because it is not the first or last time Rossi would take the lead on one of Lancaster's compositions – a move that would cause much bitterness in the years to come. Coghlan's drumming also deserves a mention here, as his signature snare fills on the back end of the track fit the groove like a hand in a glove. The song was originally supposed to fade out, but instead, the track abruptly segues into 'Don't Stop Me Now'. Careful listeners can hear the tape machine snap into 'stop mode' after Eden pressed the kill switch just as the studio take was about to end.

Not to be confused with the Queen song of the same name, 'Don't Stop Me Now' is a Lancaster and Bown composition that sits somewhere between both musicians' tastes. There's a heavy synth break and pedal tones aplenty; both hallmarks of Bown, while the lyric and riffs are unpretentious but constructive in the style of Lancaster. The pedal tone technique is a favourite of the band – usually when the bass keeps to just one note but the harmony moves around above it. The saturated guitar parts are very 'of their time' but suit the somewhat anxious track in the most Quo-like way possible.

Andrew Bown in *FTMO Magazine*, April 2021:

It's great!… Kicks bottom… I tuned the E string down to D and messed about with a riff. Went from there. Alan soon had the lyrics. Three entirely different versions – three entirely different stories. He had difficulty making his mind up sometimes… I think I've nicked a bit of that song and used it on the *Backbone* album. Sounds a little too close to 'Backing Off' for comfort.

Rossi and Frost's 'Enough is Enough' sports a bright swing feel that seems like an attempt to recapture the magic of earlier cuts like 'Down the Dustpipe' and 'Mean Girl'. It cries out for a solo from Francis, but the listener is instead treated to an organ break that sounds more like *Thomas the Tank Engine* than Andrew Bown. It's a pre-composed, repetitive break that was probably conceived by (and recorded at the behest of) Rossi and Eden. However, the track swings to an undeniable extent and doesn't let up until the fade-out.

The album closer 'Riverside' divides opinion among the fanbase due to the off-the-wall choices regarding production. The song flits between straight and swung rhythmic feels with a fade-in and fade-out on the latter – an arrangement choice made by Rossi in post-production. Originally, the track was played straight without a fade in and the shuffle feel took the track to the fade-out. To 'bookend' the track, the ending section was also copied onto the intro – the effect was achieved by crossfading with 1/4' analogue machines.

Francis Rossi:

…messy bits of tape! I was very keen on that kind of wacky experimentation at times. I'd started years back with 'Break the Rules' and such – trying to slow the tape down… put a tone on… tune to it and then… if you listen to the solo on 'Break the Rules', it's very 'arrested' so the vibrato is unnaturally fast. I was very keen to experiment with shit like that. Now I've no idea how we came across stuff like that. Bernard and I would just record things – there was no 'you can't do this!'

This Rossi/Frost composition was not recorded in Dublin with the majority of the album and was added to the tracklist at the last moment – just as the album went to be mastered. Coghlan does not remember playing drums on this cut – probably because Rossi programmed the drum parts on his Linn drum machine for his basic demo and just built the final track around it.

John Eden, posted to the *SQMB* on 12 August 2008:

> It was not a programmed drum machine, but I recall around [the time of] mixing working with Francis (as at this stage, John had left having finished all the basic drum tracks months earlier) and we added additional snare and tom fills using pretty dry sampled sounds that gave the drums a machine-like sound but manually played. Also, we had no room ambience on these dubs, which again changed the character from other tracks. There were feel issues on the basic track that these dubs were an attempt to smooth out. That's my recollection of it. With today's technology, I could have done a better job and made it sound less machine-like.

While the album has since been fairly well respected by critics and fans, Parfitt and Lancaster both have expressed a dislike of it.

John Eden posted to the *SQMB* on 1 October 2008:

> I really don't recall anyone being 'pissed off' as Alan has mentioned in an interview, and the fact that he regards *Never Too Late* as a 'throwaway' could probably just as easily be applied to *Just Supposin'*. I think these comments surround more the friction within the band rather than the actual recordings we made... Richard was going through the worst possible time any parent could imagine with the loss of Heidi when we started working on the overdubs of *Never Too Late* so it was understandable that his focus at the o/dub and mixing stage may not have been the best it could be. I think also deep down, he did not like the fact Bernie did so much of the high harmony work on these sessions, which led to his comments about people doing bit parts.

Graham Bonnet – 'Night Games'

In one of Rossi's more fruitful out-of-Quo creative partnerships, a hit record was produced with Rainbow singer Graham Bonnet. 'Night Games' was a song written by Fast Buck singer and guitarist Edwin Hamilton that is unashamedly about the red light district and paying for sex. Bonnet's manager David Oddie had the idea to bring in a famous face to produce the single to help its chances in the charts and Rossi was contacted. He took the job feeling enough self-doubt in his inexperience in the producer's chair to insist on using John Eden as his engineer and co-producer at Red Bus Studios in London. The song features an all-star band of Cozy Powell on drums, Gary Twigg on bass, Mickey Moody of Whitesnake on guitar and Andy Bown on keyboards. Rossi even contributed some rudimentary Coral Sitar for the introductory passages alongside some additional synthesiser overdubs.

Francis Rossi:

I knew Graham and liked him. He had a great voice but they always made sure he was at the top of his range all the time. It was a common thing at the time. I had to sing 'Rockin' All Over the World' at the edge of my range because they said so, so that's what we all did – same with Graham. So [for 'Night Games'] there was this dickhead from this pop band producing all these 'real' musicians and some were not having it. I was having trouble with Cozy Powell being [particularly] difficult so I asked one of them 'what's his name?… his real name…' they said 'Colin', I said (laughing) 'oh is it!?' – when I pushed the talkback button and said 'Colin!?' he politely answered 'yes?' and from then on, it was like his mum or dad was speaking to him!' It was a most enjoyable record – I loved the sequence of it, the people that played on it, it was a great little record. Shame we never got to make another one really…

What results is a number six hit record (Bonnet's biggest as a solo artist), despite *Record Mirror's* criticism that Rossi's production is 'somewhat melodramatic' – ignorant to the fact that it was recorded in one day. Rossi also produced the B-side 'Out on the Water' – a song written by Bob Young and Mickey Moody, who were working as a prolific rock duo that they established during the mid-1970s. They had released an uncharting, eponymous album in 1977 and had a handful of singles with similar commercial success, but the project was clearly a labour of love for the duo. 'Out on the Water' is a straight-ahead rocker in enough of a Quo style for Rossi to even add some of his rarely used baritone range backing vocals high up in the mix. The backing band is largely the same for this session but with Twigg replaced by Whitesnake bassist Neil Murray. Both tracks were featured on the 1981 album *Line Up* – the rest of which was produced by John Eden.

The album peaked at a disappointing number 62 – a genuine shame for a record with so much talent on it. Queen's first volume of *Greatest*

Hits was riding high at number one that November and Adam Ant's *Kings of the Wild Frontier* released the previous year, was still getting all the regular airplay. Also, The Human League's smash album *Dare* was mopping up the airtime that was left. It seems that with the public's taste changing drastically at the beginning of the decade, Bonnet's brand of rock was simply no longer in vogue.

While most of Young & Moody's creative output was tied up in the 1970s, the most curious of their releases came in 1981 when they formed a supergroup with a conglomeration of artists from rather varied backgrounds. 'Don't Do That' was a heavy rock shuffle featuring Edwin Hamilton, Cozy Powell, Lemmy Kilmister of Motorhead and the Nolan Sisters. Lemmy was known to enjoy lighter music – once citing one of his favourite records as 'You're the Reason Why' by the Rubettes. He was also enamoured by the Nolans, who were even more 'rock 'n' roll' than the boys in the band.

Unfortunately, the line-up's debut single peaked at number 63 on the UK singles chart and the group didn't collaborate again despite all speaking fondly of their time together. The duo also had a placement for their song 'These Eyes' in a Levi Jeans advert with the lyrics changed to 'Levis' with singer Graham Bonnet replacing Ed Hamilton's lead vocals for the TV version. The Quo's metaphorical family tree was clearly quite incestuous at the time.

Keyboardist Bown had had a prolific but, unfortunately, unsuccessful solo recording career alongside his session métier that started before his association with Status Quo and he released three singles as a solo artist during the 1980s. 'Say It Was Magic' was a gentle folk ballad in triple time delivered in Bown's distinctive self-effacing acuity. A prepossessing fiddle solo courtesy of later Quo collaborator Graham Preskett helps play the song out. It was backed with 'One Forward and Two Back Again' – more tuneful folk rock, which should have been a hit single of its own. It has more of Bown's hallmarks – most obviously, the shifting chords over a pedal bass note. His only other single of the 1980s would not appear until 1983.

In early December 1981, the parody band 'Status Quid' released a single, 'Boring Song' – an amusing send-up of Quo in good humour. The name was actually a sobriquet for the HeeBeeGeeBees; a band made up of comedians Angus Deayton, Michael Fenton Stevens and Philip Pope, who had a penchant for parodying popular acts of the day. It wouldn't be the last time Quo were made fun of either – Little and

Large, The Two Ronnies, and Hale and Pace, among others, would go on to poke fun at the group, with almost all of them going to great lengths to do so.

1982: 1+9+8+2

1+9+8+2

Personnel:

Francis Rossi: guitar, vocals

Rick Parfitt: guitar, vocals

Alan Lancaster: bass guitar, vocals

Pete Kircher: drums

Andy Bown: keyboards, backing vocals

Additional Musicians:

Bernie Frost: backing vocals

Produced by Status Quo

Record Label: Vertigo

Recorded: Mountain Studios, Montreux, 1982

Release date: 16 April 1982

Highest UK chart place: 1

Running time: 39:01

Side one: 'She Don't Fool Me' (Rick Parfitt, Andy Bown) – 4:36, 'Young Pretender' (Francis Rossi, Bernie Frost) – 3:34, 'Get Out and Walk' (Parfitt, Bown) – 3:13, 'Jealousy' (Rossi, Frost) – 2:55, 'I Love Rock and Roll' (Alan Lancaster) – 3:16

Side two: 'Resurrection' (Bown, Parfitt) – 3:49, 'Dear John' (John Gustafson, Jackie Macauley) – 3:14, 'Doesn't Matter' (Rossi, Frost) – 3:41, 'I Want the World to Know' (Lancaster, Keith Lamb) – 3:23, 'I Should Have Known' (Rossi, Frost) – 3:31, 'Big Man' (Lancaster, Mick Green) – 3:45

The *1+9+8+2* album was so-called to celebrate the 20-year meeting of Alan Lancaster and Francis Rossi in 1962. While *Never Too Late* had been a success, the band was in complete disarray. The amount of drug-taking, alcohol-imbibing and green-eyed jealousy around songwriting royalties had taken its toll, as tracks that were chosen as singles would pay the majority of royalties to the composers, with the performers taking a much smaller cut in comparison.

When recording began on what was to become the *1+9+8+2* album in November 1981, a pivotal moment in the band's history would occur. While the rest of the band and crew were partial to cocaine and other assorted drugs, drummer John Coghlan never partook in narcotic abuse. He preferred instead to drink copious amounts of ale that, by his own admission, would often leave him moody, confrontational and increasingly isolated from the rest of the band. Previously, he had famously walked across a large dinner table during a record company meeting when he felt like he'd heard enough business talk and become bored. When Bob Young was with the band, he would ameliorate the situation by playing the role of the mediator and advocate for the talented but unpredictable drummer. Without Young, Coghlan was paranoid, frustrated, lonely and missing his partner Gillie back home. And, as Quo were now solely self-producing for the first time since 1975's *On The Level*, there was nobody to smooth these increasingly regular situations out in the studio.

The sessions took place at Queen's Mountain studio in Montreux, Switzerland and, as usual, started with setting up the drums and getting them to sound their best. Rossi (a capable drummer himself) would tune the kit and help the engineer set up the microphones and the drums placement in the room for optimal sound quality. This tedious job would frustrate Coghlan and when he sat down at the drums to begin recording, he decided that he was not happy at all with the sound in his cans and he promptly kicked the kit over and stormed outside.

Manager Colin Johnson sent Coghlan back to the hotel and told him to prepare for his flight home to the Isle of Man. To add insult to injury, tour manager Ian Jones (with a sobriquet of the 'Axeman') was the one to actually sack Coghlan, claiming he was to be replaced with a 'drum machine'. This infuriated the drummer further and he left the band for good. Exactly how this played out is a mystery, as nobody in the band recalls the exact story in detail. What is known, however, is that Coghlan walking out of sessions and meetings was not unusual and he was normally back the next day like nothing had happened. Expecting things to blow over, the band paid it no heed and carried on working – or in Lancaster's and Parfitt's case, playing backgammon. Some say Coghlan jumped before he was pushed – others say he was outright sacked by the management. Lancaster later stated that it was Rossi who wanted the drummer gone and engineered the whole thing some time before the event occurred. One thing that does seem relatively agreed upon is that the majority of the band claim to have expected him back before the end of the recording sessions.

John Coghlan:

We'd been working so hard and been touring flat out and we were all tired… We weren't really getting on that well, really and I think we all felt [my departure] was permanent – I certainly did. I have no regrets as such, but I do remember thinking that maybe I should go back and we could talk everything through, but it never happened…

Alan Lancaster, in the *Hello Quo* documentary.

It was a big mistake getting rid of John… we only made bad albums after that…

Either way, session drummer Pete Kircher was on the next flight out to Switzerland and began recording immediately upon his arrival. Kircher had worked under producer Rossi on John Du Cann's *The World's Not Big Enough* album as a session drummer and had successful projects of his own in the form of Original Mirrors and 'I Can't Let Maggie Go' with Honeybus in 1968. He had just finished a tour with the Nolan Sisters when Rossi called him to help with the recording of the album. Kircher was delighted to be asked and was the professional, jolly and sober drummer Rossi was longing to work with. He made such an impression in Montreux that he was asked to join the band full-time.

Another change was the way Andy Bown was credited – no longer as a guest musician but as a fully-fledged member of the ensemble. This was interesting as Bown's keyboards really take centre stage on this record and Lancaster states these two massive shifts in the musical dynamic of the band to be the beginning of the end for Quo being considered a serious rock band. Once the recording was back on schedule, the band had much fun between sessions by indecorously roller-skating through the town and shooting each other with cap guns – much to the vexation of the locals.

'She Don't Fool Me' opens the album courtesy of writing team Parfitt & Bown about a relationship with a younger lover. The intro has all the hallmarks of the early '70s era band with a meticulously arranged riff for the full ensemble before the boogie groove kicks in, preceding the first verse. The words have all the zaniness of a standard Bown lyric with a catchy tune to boot, with all the vocals delivered in a perfect harmony throughout. The track is also notable for the superb piano playing on the latter half of the cut. It was the second single to be released from the album and peaked just within the top 40 at number 36.

'Young Pretender' is a bright Rossi/Frost major-key shuffle composition that has a number of ear-grabbing moments through the chord progression and a simple guitar solo performed in twin harmony. The lyrics are hard to decipher in any detail, but they are a vehicle for one of the catchiest tunes on the album. There are some questionable aesthetic sonic choices that perhaps haven't dated so well in the arrangement, but it seems in keeping with other 'pop' hits of the day. The intro features some harmonised falsetto scat singing in place of a lead instrument doubling the rhythm guitars in a homophonic fashion, and there are some examples of synthesised vocoder/talkbox lines around the pre-chorus resulting in a pure piece of pop craft.

'Get Out and Walk' is another quintessential Bown lyric composed with collaborator Rick Parfitt. It's a straight-ahead rock number that has an interesting vocal arrangement and some buried lead guitar work under the chorus. The intro features a solid guitar riff backed with a pounding backbeat from Kircher's unison snare, bass drum and floor tom and seems to be setting up a heavy Quo track as if from 1973. While the rest of the song loses this aesthetic rather quickly, it's an amusing laundry list-style song that Quo have been known to use occasionally ('Diggin Burt Bacharach' from 2002s *Heavy Traffic* is another example). It seems to be about the breaking point of a toxic relationship and is humorous and scathing in equal measure and includes the classic line 'I got fat knees from crawling so fast/I got sore lips from kissin' yo' ass'.

'Jealousy' is another earworm from Rossi & Frost and the pair would go on to re-record it as a single for their own project in 1985. The original Quo version, as found here, is a bouncy, poppy cut that features the two composers in the twin-lead-vocal role. In fact, there's more vocals recorded here than first meets the ear – there are several backing vocals recorded as overdubs – one of which features Rossi audibly saying how much he likes the song after the line 'I waste it on my own' (about 37 seconds in).

Alan Lancaster said, in an interview with Per Engelbo during 1996:

> With 'Jealousy', we played exactly the same as the demo, making it a bit better, you know. For hours and hours [Rossi] put the 'Jealousy' on that he did with Bernie Frost, and then the 'Jealousy' we did with the band. It got to the stage where I was saying to Rick 'well, we've done it exactly the same, I can't even tell which one is which now'. I believe he put on the original. I don't think that's a Status Quo-recording, 'Jealousy'. I think it's the Francis Rossi and Bernie Frost version on the album. I think if the 'Jealousy' we played was the same, he would have thrown ours off and got his on.

Keen listeners may also notice two different ride cymbals being played at the same time alongside the hi-hats and snare – evidence of Rossi's Linn drum machine being present during the overdubbing sessions for sure. Quo's version was released as a single in the Netherlands, Germany and Spain but unfortunately failed to convert itself into a hit.

In an attempt to get in on the quest for a hit song, Alan Lancaster provides us with 'I Love Rock 'n' Roll' that definitely ranks with Quo's catchiest tunes. Fans probably expected something hard-hitting from Lancaster with a title like this but were instead treated to a '50s pastiche jukebox B-side complete with slap-back echo vocals. It's not Lancaster's best-written lyric, but it does have a certain charm to the open-minded listener. The backing vocals are nicely performed and are not unlike the harmonies found on the Bluebells' 'Young at Heart' released a few years later. Lancaster harmonises with himself throughout the choruses and even throws in a couple of 'uh-huh-huh' Elvis groans in case the intention of the song wasn't clear. The song gets only slightly more harmonically adventurous over the final refrain but does leave the average fan with a small but ambivalent smile on their face. It was released as a single only in Lancaster's new home country of Australia but, like 'Jealousy', failed to chart.

The Bown and Parfitt composition 'Resurrection' is a gospel-inflected blues shuffle notable for not one but two excellent guitar solos – the first rumoured to be Parfitt, but in all likelihood, it's almost certainly Rossi playing both. It takes inspiration from 'Reason for Living' from *Hello!* (1973) in rhythm and lyrical content and 'Rocking All Over the World' in both the musical composition and structure but is a much more well-rounded, well-performed recording than the latter. The vocal arrangement adds to the gospel feel with call and response, spread sustained pads and an almost improvised, lazy feel in its delivery. Rossi's slide playing is on show here and it does not disappoint – it is laid back, cheekily melodic and full of soul.

'Dear John' was written by Roxy Music's John Gustafson and Northern Irish session musician and solo artist Jackie McAuley. It was originally conceived as a country ballad – the kind that a young James Taylor might record. When Rossi heard the demo, he decided that he should give it the Quo treatment and it was recorded for the album. 'Dear John' is a pleasant tune with a short but catchy guitar solo that was a moderate chart success for the band when released as a single in 1982, no doubt thanks to several mimed TV show appearances across Europe to promote it. It made its way into the setlist temporarily but was soon dropped for reasons unknown halfway through the short 1982 tour. It was eventually added to the 'Proposin' Medley' for the *Party Ain't Over Yet* tour in 2005 and still gets an occasional outing as part of this live collection of hits. The accompanying promo film set a precedent for the string of strange Quo attempts at a music video where the band mime to their single as if live, with storyboarded footage interspliced. In this case, a square yuppie attends a Quo concert and sees himself transformed, Cinderella-style, into a cool rocker. Not only irrelevant to the lyric, but baffling by 21st century standards.

One of the weaker cuts on the album is 'Doesn't Matter' – a Rossi/Frost contribution that appears to be about a two-timed-lover telling the other woman about the affair. It bops along harmlessly enough but is another example of Rossi's reluctance to compose riff-based songs, instead choosing to vamp around a chord or sequence to introduce the melody and lyrics. Bernie's falsetto vocals are once again present but are mixed slightly lower than usual. There's an undeniable groove set up by the bass and drums, though – a solid foundation for the thickened harmonies of the bridge and chorus sections, but the twiddly-guitar break needed to break up the slight repetitiveness alas never arrives.

'I Want the World To Know' comes from the pen of Alan Lancaster and Keith Lamb – a minor key shuffle that serves as evidence that Lancaster wanted to write material to appeal to both die-hard fans and the wider record-buying public. Rossi provides a solid solo here that is either double-tracked or dipped in analogue chorus. There are some nice rhythmic pushes scattered throughout and a close-harmony vocal arrangement that keep things interesting as the repetitive track trundles along. Lyrically, this track is a little hard to decipher but could quite easily be describing the kind of sycophantic friends one acquires as a rock star – using a little reference to 'Rockin' All Over the World'.

'I Should Have Known' is a bright shuffle brought to the album by the Rossi & Frost partnership. It stands out as an incredibly tight cut with the boogie rhythm never letting up. There are some unexpected chord changes here and the lead guitar work is some of Rossi's best ever committed to tape. Lancaster, at first, seems to shirk the full shuffle rhythm but soon lays into a tight pumping groove when the verse hits. There's a tape splice audible after the first chorus, but Kircher's simple pattern helps to not draw much attention to it. Written in the same vein as 1971's 'Mean Girl', there is an argument to suggest it was included to please older fans of the more frantic rhythms of the early band.

The album closer is something of a curiosity – a Lancaster track called 'Big Man'. It was co-written with Mick Green of 'Johnny Kidd & the Pirates' fame. The lyrics seem to support Lancaster's reputation for being a tough, 'take-no-prisoners' kind of guy but come across as naive and petulant upon first listen. However, the final verse is interesting as it addresses the idea of being replaced by someone waiting in the wings to fill your place. Perhaps Alan was preparing for his own departure from the band following Coghlan's sacking? After a simple introduction riff, the half-time verses present themselves as a nice touch, but the chorus lets the overall track down due to its repetitive lyric and a weak melody that isn't 'hooky' enough to support the words.

Another track that surfaced around this time was the Bown/Parfitt composition 'Calling the Shots'. While it didn't make the album, it was released as the B-side to 'Jealousy' and is notable for being the first time a released Quo track had featured Bown on lead vocal, and for a rare synth solo break. It's full of typical Bownisms with imagery and wordplay (including a reference to 'Falling in, Falling Out') and a loose three-part harmony with Parfitt and himself on another multi-tracked part. The tuning on some of the long sustained harmonies is a little rough around the edges but adds some welcome 'realness' to a catchy but synth-heavy cut.

Andrew Bown

'Calling The Shots'? Can't remember. Quite a good song, though. Different structure to the usual Quo stuff at the time. As for Andy Bown solo – dunno – I was trotting out a lot of stuff at the time, which could have gone either way. I mean Quo or AB.

The album topped the chart in 1982 and became Quo's fourth and final number-one album to date. While it's not much of a favourite among fans, there's a high level of musicality on it and Rossi is clearly getting more comfortable in the producer's chair by this time.

Francis Rossi in *Sounds Fan Library* Magazine in 1982:

The main thing now is to sell records and satisfy ourselves. There's lots of interesting things we can do, and maybe will do. But me? I'll just sit here and make records; that's what I'm good at and that's what I want to do…

Kircher was given the drum throne full-time; with the music press speculating that 400 applicants had expressed interest in the job (including Cozy Powell), but the impression made on the band by the ex-Shanghai drummer in Montreux had been enough to secure the job from the get-go. However, the obligatory promotional live tour was not the total success the band had hoped for their anniversary year. The shows kicked off in April in Cork, Ireland, but when the time came for their usual jaunt out of the UK and into mainland Europe, interest in booking the band had fallen due to the World Cup being held in Spain. In addition, the Rolling Stones were promoting their hugely successful *Tattoo You* album and many of the larger European venues were preparing for their arrival. Only four shows were played in Europe in 1982, in Holland, Belgium and two in Germany.

Around this time, Parfitt co-produced two singles for his wife, Marietta, with John Eden. Marietta was an acquaintance of Cliff Richard, who would occasionally attend her bible group, and so Parfitt feigned finding religion in order to meet one of his musical heroes. Cliff would go on to become friends with the pair, even contributing backing vocals to a couple of tracks recorded at Parfitt's home 24-track studio in Surrey. He's most audible on the JD Souther cover 'You're Only Lonely', but he is also apparently singing backup on 'Do You Wanna Dance?' – a song he had a hit with himself 20 years earlier. Both covers were backed with Marietta-penned originals – 'Making Up My Mind' (written with her husband and Andy Bown) and 'Only in Your Eyes I See', respectively. There's a definite attempt to keep the singer's musical aesthetic as far from her then-husband's as possible – despite some bass from Gary Twigg and drums from 10cc's Kevin Godley, most of the backing comes in the form of layered synths (surely thanks to Andy Bown) and with little to no guitar audible. Eden and Parfitt even attempted to manage Marietta under 'Parden Productions' (a portmanteau of their names), but since neither had any experience in this field, the project never yielded a hit record. Some have speculated that this recording project was an attempt to revive the pair's failing marriage that had taken a severe hit since their daughter's tragic death. The guitarist's disloyalty, alcohol intake and drug abuse were also affecting the relationship so badly that the Parfitts' nine-year marriage would come to an end when Marietta filed for divorce in 1982. While devastated by his split with Marietta (and his son through the circumstances), Parfitt would soon find himself dating Hot Gossip dancer Debbie Ash and delving deeper into his alcohol and drug addiction.

The Princes Trust

His Royal Highness, the Prince of Wales, founded the charity 'The Princes Trust' in 1976 to aid the plight of the disaffected, vulnerable and homeless youth of the UK. When funds needed to be raised in 1982, Status Quo offered their services and turned the second of two Birmingham N.E.C. shows on their anniversary tour into a charity concert. It was to be the first time a member of the royal family had officially attended a rock concert and the story made news around the world – the Elgar-loving cellist was to lose his gig virginity to Status Quo. The BBC broadcast the show live on BBC1 to an estimated 12 million viewers, but only the first half of the gig aired due to programming slots – the BBC had already moved several popular features around to accommodate it. Thankfully, it was later aired in full on BBC Radio 1's *Friday Night Rock Show* the following week. Although Princess Diana was due (and allegedly excited) to attend, being heavily pregnant with William prevented her from doing so. The Prince met the whole band and was presented with a one-off box set of all of Quo's Vertigo albums to date – the ultimate Quo rarity now resides in the vaults at Buckingham Palace but has likely never been played. After a very brief pre-recorded opening of the national anthem (6 bars in total; as is customary for a prince), Quo hit their usual setlist (including a 23-minute version of 'Forty-Five Hundred Times') and if it hadn't been for meeting the man himself beforehand (and the crowd cheering his entrance), they would have soon forgotten he was in attendance as nearly 12,000 fans rocked the night away in the established and expected fashion. The Prince stayed for the duration of the televised segment but sloped off prematurely, although he allegedly enjoyed the evening, and it was the beginning of a 30-year working relationship with the royal family and Status Quo, who would be involved in dozens of royal events for the next 30 years. The recording was released as Quo's second official live album as *Live at the N.E.C.* in 1984 and, although it didn't chart very high at number 83, the accompanying single, a live version of 'Caroline', made number 13 on the UK singles chart.

Two weeks after the successful show at the N.E.C., Quo delivered another storming set at the Rock Spektakel Festival in Dortmund Westfalenhalle, 45 minutes of which was broadcast as *Rockpop in Concert*.

Among the most interesting Quo-related appearances in 1982 was Parfitt's appearance on Rick Wakeman's TV show *Gastank* – a show that paired rock royalty with Wakeman's crack team of house band musicians to perform songs to a small studio audience. Parfitt was the first guest to ever appear on the show and despite being too drunk to remember all of the lyrics to his own compositions (and deliver the ones that he can in tune), storms through Quo favourites 'Little Lady' and 'Rain' with a quality that has been known to occasionally be missing from the Quo line up from this period. Some of Wakeman's synth interjections in lieu of lead guitar on the latter is not as palatable as it was at the time but still contributes to the Parfitt-led band in showcasing the collective musicianship in the room. Seeing Parfitt in the musical director's role is quite something to behold – he's confident, decisive and clearly in his comfort zone. When asked about the next twelve months for the 1982 tour programme, Lancaster and Parfitt explained:

Lancaster:

There is talk of aiming at the US market… we make the music, and it's up to us whether we bring in a producer for the next album to try and get the sound that will break it… it's not a major worry the way I see it. But what is important, and will be for the years to come, is how happy Quo are within themselves at the moment…

Parfitt:

At the moment it's a happy medium. Everyone is doing their thing just outside Quo, but the main thing is the band. That's the core for all five of us, and it stems out from there.

1983: Back to Back

Back to Back

Personnel:

Francis Rossi: guitar, vocals

Rick Parfitt: guitar, vocals

Alan Lancaster: bass guitar, vocals

Pete Kircher: drums, backing vocals

Andy Bown: keyboards, backing vocals

Additional Musicians:

Bernie Frost: backing vocals

Produced by Status Quo

Record Label: Vertigo

Recorded: AIR Studios, Montserrat, 1983

Release date: 25 November 1983

Highest UK chart place: 9

Running time: 32:55

Side one: 'A Mess of Blues' (Doc Pomus, Mort Shuman) – 3:23, 'Ol' Rag Blues' (Alan Lancaster, Keith Lamb) – 2:51, 'Can't Be Done' (Francis Rossi, Bernie Frost) – 3:07, 'Too Close to the Ground' (Rick Parfitt, Andrew Bown) - 3:43, 'No Contract' (Rick Parfitt, Andrew Bown) – 3:40

Side two: 'Win or Lose' (Francis Rossi, Bernie Frost) – 2:35, 'Marguerita Time' (Francis Rossi, Bernie Frost) - 3:27, 'Your Kind of Love' (Alan Lancaster, Ferguson Skinner) – 3:24, 'Stay the Night' (Francis Rossi, Bernie Frost, Andrew Miller) - 3:02, 'Going Down Town Tonight' (Guy Johnson) – 3:33

The final studio album to feature Alan Lancaster as a member of Status Quo came in the form of 1983's *Back to Back*. It was recorded over eight weeks starting in the February of 1983 at AIR Studios in Montserrat – a studio at the time owned by 'fifth Beatle' George Martin. With a working title of 'Round One', the band spent more money on this album than any previous effort and yet none of them seemed pleased with the end result. The location, weather and access to alcohol served as the three main barriers to work, as most of the time on the Caribbean island was spent socialising and relaxing. While most of the band blamed the lacklustre work ethic for the mixed bag of finished recordings, Rossi maintains that the real issue was the sound of the studio and equipment not being right for Quo. The recordings were so disappointing upon hearing them back in the UK that elements of the songs were re-recorded at The Factory studios in Woldingham in order to add some grit to them. The album's eventual release resulted in a number nine hit for the band but was the last to feature Lancaster or Kircher as current studio members of Status Quo.

It's important to note that Martin's studio was equipped with state-of-the-art technology and was judiciously respected by several major artists of the '70s and '80s, including The Police, Dire Straits and Duran Duran. Reading between the lines, it seems that experienced producer Rossi isn't criticising the studio itself but Quo's decision to use the technology to modernise the sonic architecture of the band for commercial purposes. Other rock albums from the same year include Def Leppard's *Pyromania*, *Synchronicity* by the Police and *Eliminator* by ZZ Top – all hit albums with just the right amount of rock swagger to counterbalance the slick, modern, hi-fi production. The trouble with Quo was that the sound they ended up with at AIR was pristine, safe and only relatively commercial – all characteristics the band were trying to escape musically but simultaneously chasing in order to stay relevant in the changing scenes of the popular music world. Quo were old-school and were never quick enough off the mark to keep up-to-date with trends in pop music production. They had learned to make records the same way the Beatles and Stones did. When those musicians wanted a trend-setting sound later in their careers, they hired the best new producers and engineers to help. Quo were self-producing and doing a good job of it too, but were using sounds and ideas two years out of date which, to the record buying public of the 80s, may as well have been a lifetime.

As if this dichotomy wasn't enough of a hurdle, individual members were pulling the creative output of the band in different directions too. Lancaster felt that he and Parfitt wanted to keep the band exploring the rockier side of their skill set, but Rossi wanted to maintain the band's reputation as a hit-making machine, whatever the cost to Quo's hard-won hard rock integrity. While Bown and Kircher were considered full-time members of the band by this point, they may have still felt like employees and, according to Lancaster, almost always sided with Rossi when a disagreement arose. Outnumbered, Lancaster and Parfitt valiantly tried to bridge the gap between commercial pop and hard rock but to little avail. Even more so than its predecessor, this album was responsible for the break-up of Status Quo.

The sleeve design was the brainchild of manager Colin Johnson – two British Leyland trucks side-by-side (or back-to-back) photographed by Bob

Elsdale with the reflective, mirror theme echoed on the back in a photo taken by Johnson himself.

The album opens with a cover version of Pomus & Shuman's 'Mess of Blues' presented as a swinging shuffle with an undeniable laid-back feel that Quo were, by now, experts at. The opening guitar break and later solos are accurate and deliberate in a way that Rossi's improvised lines occasionally lacked during this period. The vocals are harmonised in a tight, improvised three-part arrangement with Rossi backed up by Parfitt's chest voice below and Bernie Frost above the melody in head voice. Parfitt's backing vocal is mixed incredibly low here – a much more frequent occurrence since Frost's involvement in the recording process. The song was released as the second single from the album, backed with *1+9+8+2*'s 'Big Man' and reached a respectable number 15 in the UK singles chart. Because Lancaster refused to leave his pregnant wife's side in Australia, the band had to film several pre-planned promotional shoots without him. He eventually took legal action against the band to ensure they would be unable to appear without him in future without his written consent. This would be a sign of things to come and caused friction between the bassist, the band, and their management.

'Ol' Rag Blues' is one of the two offending songs from the album that ruined whatever remaining friendship Rossi and Lancaster shared in the early '80s. It's arguably the best attempt on the album to provide a rock song in a commercial setting but was tortured by internal and external politics. Written by Lancaster and collaborator Keith Lamb, this rhythmically straight, middle-of-the-road tune features some simple but surprising harmonic moments that make this a song as far from Quo-by-numbers as almost any other cut on the record. Rossi's lead guitar breaks are inspiringly melodic, expertly executed and exquisitely accompanied by the full band on top form. Curiously, several different versions exist of what sounds like a finished recording. Lancaster sang the original lead vocal in Montserrat. When Vertigo's Brian Sheppard heard the song, he liked its chances as a single but would only sanction its release if Rossi replaced Lancaster's vocal. Lancaster had sung lead vocal on several Quo album tracks and B sides but never an A-side single (one notable exception being a lead vocal shared with Rossi on 'Hurdy Gurdy Man' – a Lancaster song released by Quo precursor The Spectres in 1966 that failed to chart). Lancaster's voice had not been deemed commercial enough now that the public associated the sound of Quo with Rossi and Parfitt's vocals. The bassist and composer claimed that Rossi broke a promise by going behind his back, hogging the spotlight and not standing by his old friend – an account that Rossi fervently disputes. Rossi (and the evidence) suggests that two lead vocals were recorded – one with Rossi, one with Lancaster and the record company making the executive decision on which to release. Unsurprisingly, they went with Rossi's take with Rick Parfitt singing the bridge section for good measure. It was a wise move as far as commercial success was concerned, as it hit number nine on the UK singles chart as the first single from the album in September 1983, but it left Lancaster feeling even more jaded and ostracised than ever before.

Track three is a Rossi and Frost composition named 'Can't Be Done'. It's a catchy ear-worm of a groove but with no real instrumental hooks to speak of. It's one of the band's ubiquitous shuffles that does prompt a head bob or two with the help of Kircher's four-on-the-floor beat. Frost provides harmony vocals from beginning to end – a blend that Rossi was becoming more fond of with every song cut. Some of Frost's soon-to-be trademark 'woo-hoo' backing figures are present throughout the guitar solo, too but mixed low enough to be barely audible to only the keenest listener.

'Too Close to the Ground' is a country ballad in 12/8 time that has not only some of Quo's best lyrics to date (courtesy of Bown and, if the *Just for The Record* 1993 book is to be believed, Parfitt), but also a beautiful synthesised string part in the second verse that could only have been slightly improved with a real string section. Although not a Rossi song, it's sung by him and totally solo (although double-tracked in places). Rick was originally quite upset that Francis decided to sing lead vocals on it but was pleased with the finished result. It's by far the most honest, emotional song on the record and shows off the lyrical prowess of Bown as the main composer, and it has the keyboardist's exquisite harmonic vocabulary weaved through it. The lyrics could quite easily be describing Parfitt's mental health at the time – Bown would often compose songs inspired by or for his friends, such as 'Rock n Roll Baby Blues', 'Ruby and Roy' and sometimes with the true meaning totally disguised as in 1994's 'Confidence'. 'Too Close to the Ground' was intended to be a single but was later flipped to become a B-side to the final single from the album 'Going Down Town Tonight'.

Andrew Bown:

Francis loved it. He pushed very hard for it to be a single but… I played it the other day and he did a fabulous vocal on it. One of his very best, in my opinion. Looking back, it could either have done spectacularly well or completely stiffed. Anyway, the record company bottled out as I recall. I'm afraid Richard had nothing to do with that one either – but it was always swings and roundabouts on the writing front – and if I started something by myself, I usually just didn't stop until it was cooked.

Rossi's guitar solo is accompanied by a slow, throbbing, bluesy shuffle and a snare sound that could be mistaken for a Smith & Wesson fired in a sea cave. It has since become fairly common knowledge among the fanbase that the finished writing credits are often inaccurate. Even Quo's 1979 monster hit 'Whatever You Want' was credited to Parfitt despite him not contributing anything to the song besides the classic (but unrelated) slow introduction. Lancaster has also since claimed that the writing credits (especially from the 1970s) were unreliable in an interview with 'Backwater' – a Swedish fanclub newsletter.

Side one concludes with a Bown & Parfitt composition, 'No Contract'. The lyrics seemingly depict a casual relationship with the protagonist, preferring to keep things simple and without obligations. There's elements of heavy metal here – especially in the flanged rhythm guitar part courtesy of Parfitt's 'Electric Mistress' pedal. The track opens with a simple riff played in parallel fourths (akin to that of Deep Purple's 'Smoke on the Water') before the band crashes in to accompany a gritty vocal from Parfitt. Lancaster plays some occasional melodic material around his pumping roots and gives the track its groove. It is an attempt at bringing the average 'heaviness' of the album up but to no avail. It seems that musical director Rossi and his sideman Frost wanted to keep pursuing the commercial pop sound that was more likely to spawn their next hit single than rehash the raw sound of previous Quo recordings.

Side two opens with 'Win or Lose' – a Rossi and Frost piece that features both singers in their trademark two-part almost completely throughout. It was originally recorded as a single by UK punk harmonicist Lew Lewis in 1979 but never yielded a hit for either act. The track is faster than most of the others on the album and would have probably been a hit for a country band like Alabama. The chorus is melodious but not particularly thought-provoking. The contextual detail is added in the verses and describes some kind of escape from a relationship or situation but without any real reference as to what. The track lacks a guitar solo – relying instead on a four-bar, double-tracked lead break used throughout the song.

The next song, a country-flavoured shuffle, is regarded by many as the proverbial straw that broke the camel's back. 'Marguerita Time' was a Rossi and Frost composition that bears hardly any resemblance to the Quo singles of the 1970s. Rossi began writing the song on the piano at home before taking the basic skeleton of the composition to Frost a short while later. It features a Tin Pan Alley-esque melody that would have suited the pub sing-alongs of the 1940s and a synthesised fiddle sound that would have suited a computer game from the 1980s. The sound came from a Roland VP 330 synthesiser that Rossi was introduced to at a trade show at Earls Court a few years earlier. The idea to use the relatively new machine came from engineer Tim Summerhayes and, although there are plenty of layered acoustic guitars at front and centre, there's a subtly driven electric or two in the mix also that were recorded through an orange Roland cube amplifier just outside the control room door at The Factory. Ironically, for a song he would claim to loathe, Lancaster's bass line is quite inventive here – it's full of space and is both harmonically complete and introduces each chord change in an almost 'Jamerson-esque' fashion, but it was conceived by Bown and Rossi and taught to Lancaster while overdubbing. While it proves that Lancaster wasn't just a rock bassist at all and was, in fact, much more versatile than he would have people believe, he allegedly simply struggled to see the benefit of playing in such a fashion. At the time, Rossi had been exposed to the tequila-based cocktail by Queen in a restaurant in Montreux a few years earlier and eventually used it to feed his increasingly dangerous alcohol addiction. When the band were asked to record it, Lancaster was under the impression that this was to be a demo for Rossi and Frost's upcoming (and later abandoned) solo project 'Flying Debris' and so he kept his opinion of the song quiet, to begin with. When he found out that it was to be included on the next Quo album and released as a single, he was furious and was so embarrassed by the record that he claimed that he couldn't even face his family and friends. It flew in the face of everything he wanted Status Quo to be and was so embarrassed by the sound of the recording that he refused to appear in any of the promotional material for it, turning down dozens of TV appearances and the cabaret-tinged official promo video directed by Nigel Dick, filmed at the Sheraton Skyline Hotel in Heathrow.

Francis Rossi:

In the video, there's a girl in the middle [instrumental section] with these little round, Lennon, black glasses and just swings from left to right… and there's such happiness in the shot.

Lancaster did however appear in the *TOTP* Christmas special in 1983 but looks like he'd rather be anywhere else – and he was for the follow-up appearance in January 1984. This particular mimed performance is famous for two reasons: one, that Slade's Jim Lea stood in for Lancaster who refused to appear in any more 'Marguerita Time' promotion and two, Rick Parfitt (allegedly on purpose) walks into the drum kit sending him, Kircher and the whole gallimaufry of drums rolling into the audience. Lancaster was also absent from the infamous appearance on the *Cannon & Ball* show in 1983, which was probably a good idea as he probably would not have approved of being manhandled by the comedy duo as Rossi and Parfitt were as part of the introduction skit. The leaving of the not-so-loyal fanbase allowed Rossi and Parfitt to become light entertainment TV personalities – a double-act that was entertaining, funny and far away from their unwashed, grungy bad-boy appearance they were originally famous for.

Francis Rossi in the *Hello Quo* documentary:

> Rick didn't want to do ['Marguerita Time'] either. We were about to have dinner in Montserrat [when Alan suggested we record it], but he kind of put it down as something that wasn't going to be used.

'Marguerita Time' gave Quo a number three hit and any hardcore fans that were lost as a result were simultaneously replaced by casual listeners looking for a new catchy record to buy. The song was covered by Dexy's Midnight Runners as a B-side to 'This is What She's Like' from 1985 – Dexy's Midnight Runners also have another connection to Quo that would not come to light until 1986. Rossi has always staunchly defended the song and despite the animosity involved in the making, promotion and success of this hit single, Rossi still names it as his favourite Quo record of all time.

Francis Rossi:

> There are a few records that I've done over the years that I don't care if other people like them – most of the time, you want people to like your songs, your record, your album, whatever it is, and there are others where I really don't give a shit…

Lancaster tries to claw back some macho credibility with the next cut, 'Your Kind of Love' – a track written with fellow Aussie and session musician David Skinner. Skinner is known for working with Roxy Music and for multiple TV companies scoring to picture. There's a beautifully honky bass high in the mix that drives the surprisingly simple but uncharacteristic chord sequence along. Lancaster was himself clearly trying to pen a hit single, and although it isn't anywhere near as good as 'Ol' Rag Blues', it is undeniably commercial-sounding with a sweet solo from Rossi and call and response vocals with Parfitt high in the backing vocal mix. The composer delivers a dynamic double-tracked vocal that really builds in intensity as the track plays. The vocal arrangement gets increasingly thicker with overdubbed harmonies until the fade out.

Another Rossi/Frost composition holds the penultimate spot on the collection and is possibly among the best album tracks that the duo composed together. It was written in conjunction with Andrew Miller – a respected engineer who worked on a couple of Quo's mid-70s albums. On 'Stay the Night', Lancaster provides some lightly syncopated grooves with lots of space – often doubling Kircher's bass drum. The lyrics are fairly self-explanatory and don't require much decoding. It's hard to imagine any other act recording this song – it's one of many artefacts that proves Status Quo's commercial sound as a genre-defying mélange of excellent musicianship, catchy tunes, questionable aesthetic and production choices and country rock overtones.

The album's closer 'Going Down Town Tonight' was recorded twice and, according to Lancaster, neither version featured any member of Status Quo except Rossi. The song was brought to Rossi's attention when the song's composer Guy Johnson suggested it as a potential Quo single. Whether the backing track was the original demo that Rossi replaced the vocals on or the whole instrumental was recorded by Rossi in Montserrat has never been confirmed. What is known is that the two released versions (an album version and a single version) are recorded in two different keys, with the latter featuring one of Rossi's best guitar solos on record, where the album version has none. The original album version was recorded in C major, with the single version playing in D-flat. There is evidence to suggest that the single version instrumental was simply pitched up using Varispeed, had the vocals re-recorded and the extra space made for the solo using a tape edit. Close inspection of the bass line reveals it's definitely played with a plectrum, but the notes are even shorter than Lancaster usually plays. Rossi's plectrum bass playing has been known to feature very staccato notes to keep the bottom-end tidy. A *TOTP* appearance showed the band miming and going through the motions with what looks like borrowed equipment to pose with, but despite an amusing cartoon cover hand-drawn by Rob Fletcher (collaborator to Bob Young) and an equally amusing promotional video of the cohorts larking around on tour, the single failed to reach higher than a modest number 20 in the UK chart.

Francis Rossi:

> I got talked into that one. There was a songwriter who came to my house when he was 19 – a delightful fellow, his name was Guy Johnson... he wrote some brilliant stuff. He had these lovely demos and he had a way with him... he was really ultra-commercial. He was a classical pianist which was weird... One of the management coerced me into believing we needed this fucking track. When I finished [singing on] the track, it was a really amateurish-sounding production, but now I hear it, it's just got something about it.

The album represents the end of an era for Quo's recording career. Although another incarnation of the band would successfully take up the mantle in a few years, this would be the last studio album to feature Kircher and founding member Lancaster. Despite giving the band yet another gold disc to add to their now rather large collection, the reviews were ambivalent at best and the opinions of the purists within the Frantic Four fanbase were not quite as polite. The album has its high points – the singles and 'Too Close to the Ground' in particular, but the project as a whole feels like five people pulling in separate directions, yet all of them wanting hits. The incongruous tracklist and heterogeneous production styles left both the band, fanbase and critics despondent.

Alan Lancaster in *Back to Back* Deluxe Edition CD liner notes:

> Because we had become so separate from one another, it was hard to blend our ideas like we had in the past. Status Quo was an organic, spiritual band – but you had to work at it together, and that wasn't happening anymore.

Bown's final solo single of the 1980s was an obscure track titled 'Help Me'. It was recorded at Surrey Sound Studios with bassist Gary Tibbs (of Roxy Music, Adam and the Ants), session ace Phil Palmer on guitar and Stewart Copeland of the Police on drums. It was produced by studio

founder Nigel Gray and released in 1983. The song features Bo
archetypal lyric writing and ear-grabbing harmonic movements
Copeland's unique drumming is the main point of interest; his ...
hi-hat flourishes and pulsing double-time grooves had already become
two of his signature musical characteristics. The lyrics are about the
horrors of paying tax as a high earner in the 1980s, albeit delivered in a
humorous fashion. It was backed with 'Marianne' – a song that had been
released as an A-side the year before. The track is an acoustic folk-rock
ballad featuring bubbling organ licks and one of Bown's strongest lead
vocals on record.

Andrew Bown:

'One Forward' and 'Marianne' were recorded at Surrey Sound in
Leatherhead with Nigel Gray RIP — I spent a lot of time there. We'd mess
around all night sometimes, and of course, it was usually rubbish in the
cold light of day. That's also where we recorded 'Help Me', which is one
of the few records of mine of which I'm still proud. And we just asked a
few nice people to come along for a few hours and play a bit. Obviously,
Nigel knew Stewart Copeland, having produced the first three Police
albums, and I'd done loads of work with the lovely Phil Palmer.

Known to few outside of the Floyd fanbase, Bown also contributed
keyboards to six of the twelve tracks on Pink Floyd's The *Final Cut*
album released in 1983. While the album peaked at number one in the
UK, it took several years for the artistic quality of the record to be fairly
recognised and is now considered by some fans of the progressive rockers
to be the 'last great Pink Floyd album'.

Rick spent several weeks writing with Thin Lizzy's Phil Lynott around
this time too. Three songs were known to have been written, but the
details around where, when and the strength of Parfitt's contributions are
hazy. None of these songs ever got past the demo stages but have since
become available as bootleg releases thanks to the benevolent internet
fanbase of both artists.

'She Got Class' is a fast boogie shuffle that has a solid nucleus of an
idea but is quite obviously unfinished. 'Father of My Son' is a much more
fleshed-out composition but is still accompanied by a thin arrangement
consisting of drum machine and a distinct lack of bass frequencies due to
being recorded straight to cassette. 'Bad Boy' is the best song here as far
as production value is concerned but still lacks a finished arrangement. It

shows Parfitt's rhythm guitar on full throttle, albeit with a weedy tone and little regard for variation.

Another track originally attributed to the pair has since been refuted by several Lynott aficionados stating that 'Kill' was neither written with Parfitt nor features his guitar playing but was in fact, Snowy White, albeit playing in a style reminiscent of Parfitt.

Appraising these recordings in this manner is probably unfair as they are artefacts of writing sessions – not recording sessions and despite what some bootlegs label them as, definitely not studio demos but reference recordings made at home, probably made after several drinks and various other substances were imbibed.

1984: The End of the Road

With the tensions in the band becoming increasingly untenable, Rossi decided to fold Status Quo as a touring act; the plan was to focus on putting out records in the same way the Beatles had done in 1966. As he later recalled in the *Hello Quo* documentary in 2012, 'The end of the road, but still making tracks'.

Alan Lancaster in an unknown radio interview in 1984, said:

We've done more live shows than any other band that I know of… but these days, it's not so necessary to tour. We're all a little bit older now, we all have family ties… and the band still get on socially but musically and business-wise, we're a disaster. So we're in the process of making that side better… we've got to work in a deeper way. We've got to get into the studio side a bit more – the technical side, which is very difficult for us because we're mainly a live band.

While no tour took place in 1983, the short months the band were together recording and promoting *Back to Back* were enough to drive a wedge between Francis and Alan that would not be reconciled for around 30 years.

The fans were not given a full explanation of how this new setup would happen (or even why this was happening), but they knew that Rossi's musical proclivities were now at total odds with founding member Lancaster's – but all interviews from the time barely even hint at the real reason behind the breakup.

Alan Lancaster speaking again in 1984:

The main reason is that we've had enough touring. It seems to be a lot of wasted life, touring around the world. It's fun when you first start out, the first few years… you get to love it. But after you've been doing it as long as us, it becomes routine; you've done it all before. It's the same places, same countries, same trip, the same routine…

While Parfitt was left to play powerless umpire, Bown and Kircher were left as semi-employed bystanders, unsure of their future with the band. Lancaster was keen to develop the band's 'studio technique' and reassured fans that bigger, better records would be forthcoming. With one notable exception, this plan did not materialise.

Francis Rossi, in a Youngline RTÉ interview in Dublin in 1984:

> [We're stopping now] because we're riding on the crest of a wave and we might not for much longer. We don't want to go down and then say goodbye. We'd rather go out now so that at least people can say 'they went out and they were still good…

Rossi's relationship with Alan now seemed so dire that the pair had to force smiles at each other on stage to keep up appearances. The 69-date 'End of the Road' tour began in Dublin on 11 April and finished at Milton Keynes Bowl on 21 July of the same year. No support band opened for Quo on this tour with the exception of the final show that was opened by Gary Glitter, Nazareth, Marillion and Jason & the Scorchers. While the gig was considered to be a roaring success, the band (Parfitt in particular) found the day so bitterly emotional that he found no enjoyment in the love shown by the 35,000 fans who travelled from all across the globe to witness it. The tour's two-and-a-half-hour setlist was filled with hit singles and fan-favourite album tracks. No songs from the last album were performed live – mainly due to the fact that this tour was about thanking the fans and banking some retirement money for the band who were about to go their separate ways. Other notable dates included the penultimate show at Crystal Palace, Selhurst Park on 14 July (with Chas & Dave, Dave Edmunds, Little Steven & the Disciples of Soul and Phil Lynott's Grand Slam as support) and two nights at the Glasgow Apollo (the venue where Quo recorded their famous *Live!* album during the 1976 *Blue For You* tour) and seven consecutive nights at London's Hammersmith Apollo.

On the afternoon of the first Glasgow Apollo show in 1984, Parfitt, Rossi and Lancaster were interviewed by Scottish Television. Parfitt mused, 'We've always had an affinity with the fans up here. They're a loud lot, but a good lot. We always look forward to doing the Green's Playhouse'.

Bob Young even made his first stage appearances as harmonicist with the band since 1979's *If You Can't Stand the Heat* tour on the final two shows in 1984. The boat had well and truly been pushed out; the band were even flown in by helicopter for the final show making for a rock-star entrance that few other successful bands ever get to experience.

Pete Kircher in *Again and Again* by Bob Young and John Sherlaw:

> I won't mind being off the road at all, in fact, I'd more or less resigned myself to it anyway before I joined Quo. I suppose it'll give me more time

to work on my house… Besides, I'll be pushing 40 soon and is that ever too old to be a rock drummer? I've enjoyed it all, except for the odd bits in between when I used to think, 'Am I in the band or not?'…

Rick Parfitt in the *Hello Quo* Documentary:

> I remember being on the stage at Milton Keynes there thinking, 'we've finished 'Caroline' – God, that's the last time I'm ever gonna play that' and 'Forty-Five Hundred Times', all that… I'm never gonna play this again.

Rossi was becoming so exhausted and inebriated with tequila and cocaine that several European dates had to be cancelled after he collapsed at a show in Switzerland. The final Milton Keynes Bowl gig was filmed for VHS release, but the audio was heavily doctored by the band afterwards to fix not only the overall mix but the shabby, drunken performance – especially in Rick and Francis' vocals that were totally re-recorded due to issues with tuning and forgetting lyrics. At these mixing sessions (again at The Factory in Surrey), the band were back at least on speaking terms and are said to have enjoyed each other's company so much that they agreed to shoot a low-budget video for what would be the line-up's final single release.

'The Wanderer' was a number 11 hit record for the quintet in the autumn of 1984 – despite being a cover version of the classic 1961 record by Dion. Whilst it wasn't uncommon for Quo to record cover versions from time to time, it was a strange choice as the first (and last) single of the newly 'road-retired' band. Produced by Pip Williams (presumably to add some professional sparkle to the finished product) at RAK Studios in London, the record featured Rossi on lead vocal (mixed surprisingly high for a Quo record) with Parfitt singing harmony and eventually lead vocal on the bridge sections.

Francis Rossi:

> I was doing the vocal on that, singing away, and I could see everyone looking through the [control room] glass… going around the studio… changing the microphones… changing the cables… checking the patch bay… then the engineer spotted that when I was singing 'around, around, around', one of my teeth was touching another tooth and making a [buzzing sound].

The record also features legendary UK jazz saxophonist Dick Morrissey on tenor saxophone – most likely recruited for the session by Williams. A video directed by Sebastian Harris was filmed around London with the band miming to their new record on an open flatbed truck with most of their stage equipment. The musicians were taped onto vertical poles for safety. Passers-by look bemused, thrilled, and irritated in equal measure.

Rick Parfitt in *Down Down Through the Decades:*

> That started out as a great day… we thought, 'what a great, basic idea'. I found it a bit embarrassing but it created so much interest through the City of London – people hanging out of windows [wondering] 'what the fuck is that?!'.

Interesting to note that there is no trace of Frost on the audio or visual recording, probably due to Francis now trying to keep the two acts as separate entities. Having a vehicle for his lighter material in his duo project, Francis was probably happy to revisit a slightly rockier sound with Quo. British comedy duo 'The Two Ronnies' parodied the song in March 1985 for their sketch show on BBC1 – the resulting recording (titled 'Very Fond Of Her') was so amusing to Rossi and Parfitt that they would occasionally change the lyrics of the Wanderer in live performances to those written by Barker and Corbett.

Quo recorded other songs around the same time, including the Bruce Springsteen song 'Cadillac Ranch' – recorded by Quo around the same time as 'The Wanderer' at the behest of manager Colin Johnson as he believed it could help break Quo into America. Quo's recording is a faithful reproduction of the Springsteen original and does suit the band's light-rock aesthetic. Intended for the untitled album that would never come to fruition, it remained largely unheard for decades until it was released officially as part of a box set in 2001 and later on CD reissues of the *Back to Back* album.

For Rossi, any further plans being made for Status Quo inside or outside of the studio were mostly academic – he felt he could no longer work within the constraints of the Quo brand and more so, that of bassist Lancaster. When asked about reforming, he said:

Francis Rossi in the End of the Road souvenir magazine:

> Ah no, I think that's nasty. I always used to hate that – various bands did that in the '70s, split up and reformed, it was kinda groovy, it revamped

the interest... Quo won't be doing that – however bad the money situation is! It really pisses me off when people say they wanna get back to their roots and all that shite, you know, the club circuit... they're just lying...

Unfortunately for Rossi, Status Quo would end up doing both.

Rossi & Frost – Flying Debris

As Status Quo were winding down, Rossi and Frost were gearing up for their debut album as a duo. The Vertigo-funded *Flying Debris* album (with a working title of 'Far and Wide') was scheduled to be Rossi's return to the charts, but this time, without the constraints of pleasing a pre-existing fanbase. The debut single was 'Modern Romance' – a straight quaver country track written by the duo and released in March 1985 that featured Frost's first solo vocal passage on the bridge section. The song is totally free of the boogying guitars and reprises the synthesised fiddle sound of 'Marguerita Time'. It's a likeable recording that makes the most of the pair's vocal blend and predilection for hummable melodies.

Francis Rossi:

I thought ['Modern Romance'] was excellent. There was a band called Modern Romance, there was just a whole thing about modern romance [at the time]. It got panned because you're expected to do something 'rawk', and the minute you step out of that...! In the end, what we like about ourselves, isn't what the punters see...

A low-budget video starring a young Samantha Fox and a slightly older, pipe-smoking Peter Richardson was filmed on a building-site set with the songwriters awkwardly accompanying the scenes. Unfortunately, no high-quality footage exists and the only way of knowing the video even exists is by trawling YouTube for home-recorded footage from the early 1980s. The song was backed with another Rossi/Frost penned song, 'I Wonder Why'; a fast-paced, synth-heavy rock song that still had elements of the pair's melodic trademarks but lacked the country flavour that the A-side had in abundance. The drum machine and synth bass hammer away with little variation – the only traditional Quo-related instrument at front and centre being the human voices of the composers. The single just missed out on a top 50 spot (peaking at number 54 on the UK Singles Chart), but a follow-up single was released in October 1985 that unfortunately fared even worse. A faithful re-recording of 'Jealousy' was released with a green-eyed woman on the cover. The A-side features some extra synthesised layers that were more than likely done with an arpeggiator. There's a breakdown section that brings an off-beat accordion to the foreground that isn't audible on the original *1+9+8+2* cut. The song was backed with 'Where Are You Now?' – a rock shuffle written by Rossi and Frost that features not only a tidy vocal arrangement but also some creative lead guitar playing from Rossi. Like 'Jealousy', this song also features the singers in harmony throughout but with Frost contributing his falsetto counterlines to certain sections. Some unison 'oohs' join the refrain for the fade-out. Some 12" releases saw an extra track added to the previous two in the form of 'That's Alright'. A re-recorded version of this track was used as a B-side to 'Ain't Complaining' some years later but had credited Parfitt as a third composer – but strangely, the PRS database does not list Parfitt as a composer of this work in either of its forms. The original recording is a sultry shuffle that, while lacking some bottom end, definitely inspires a foot-tap or head bob. The synthesised baritone saxophone (panned slightly left) and keyboard interjections and pitch-shifted vocals haven't dated particularly well, but the record served as a more than adequate demo to the far superior later version produced by Pip Williams at Chipping Norton. 'Jealousy' peaked at number 98 on the UK Singles Chart. Both musicians were disappointed in the chart positions of both singles, to say the least, but Rossi took this comparable failure particularly hard as he now realised that he had walked away from the band (and brand) that had helped propel his records to success.

Rossi has since claimed that part of this failure was due to Frost not feeling or looking comfortable filling Parfitt's shoes as Rossi's right-hand man. While this alone would not have necessarily accounted for the lack of sales, it could have played a part in new audiences feeling confused by the new face next to Francis Rossi. Playback performances or interviews on the likes of *Cheggers Plays Pop*, Dutch programme *Pop Shjop*, the *Wide Awake Show* and the *Wogan Show* (featuring Andy Bown on bass and Pete Kircher on drums – it is unclear as to whether these musicians actually played on the record) did little to cement Frost's reputation as a strong stage presence next to his co-star.

Consequently, Vertigo rather heavy-handedly decided to hold back on the release of the album for fear of ploughing any more money into a duo showing little to no promise in terms of record sales.

As a result, a complete track listing for the shelved *Flying Debris* al. has only ever been speculated about among collectors of bootlegs and rarities.

It's unlikely that any older Frost material (produced by Rossi or otherwise) would have been included as it would not have fit aesthetically and had already been released anyway. Other than the two singles and the five B-sides, nothing else from these Rossi & Frost sessions has seen the light of day, although it is possible that a Rossi & Frost song titled 'Billy' was written around this time. This song (although never even recorded by the pair) was inspired by a dog of the same name belonging to Rossi's then-partner Elizabeth Gernon and would have been a bright, major key shuffle had it made it to the studio, and the 'it will make my day to be with you' refrain would have satisfied fans of the lighter, poppier side of Francis Rossi.

The pair's composition 'Isaac Ryan' (a play on 'eyes are crying') would also be a strong contender to be an album track. Rossi would eventually record this song for his debut 1996 solo album 'King of the Doghouse'. When the original track was recorded, Rossi and Frost played it for Lancaster in the car…

Francis Rossi:

He [Lancaster] said 'it's really good, that, but it needs a 'man's' bass on it though…' because the bass was a kind of root and fifth basically; and the same when we were doing 'Marguerita'… – it was Andrew Bown that kinda went through [the bass parts] and it was the three of us in the control room trying to get Alan to do [the descending bass line], but again, a root and fifth-ish bass and I think Alan believed… 'no-one's ever gonna get that released'…

Alan Lancaster, in a 1996 Interview with Per Engelbo, said:

Oh yes, Francis and I sat in his BMW and he played the whole album to me. We sat there, and I said, 'good one there, Francis, you need a little work here…'. His stuff, in fact, had a certain little bit of charm, good bits here and there.

The original 1980s recording of the song has never been publicly released and, according to Rossi, may have actually been lost along with the rest of the tapes.

Recorded Delivery

le, was busy making his own solo record and working
projects. He was recruited by Queen's drummer Roger
actor-turned-singer Jimmy Nail's debut single – a cover
ard 'Love Don't Live Here Anymore' originally recorded
by Rose Royce. The track was co-produced by Taylor and hit number three
on the UK singles chart in the spring of 1985. Parfitt had also co-written
and played on a track from Taylor's 1984 album *Strange Frontier*. 'It's An
Illusion' even features Parfitt on backing vocals and is among the stronger
tracks on the album.

Alan Lancaster talking to Per Engelbo:

> I was living with Rick for a while, so all I got to hear then, day in and day
> out, was his solo album... Compared with Francis' stuff, Rick's material
> was more earthy. It had good bits too, but that's not good enough, you
> know. When I came over with my stuff, the record company didn't even
> want to give me a deal. They had just spent £100,000 pounds on Francis,
> and £100,000 pounds on Rick, and they came up with absolutely...
> nothing!

Parfitt's solo album *Recorded Delivery* was produced by old Quo
collaborator Pip Williams. Williams had been working with Norwegian
singer Trond Granlund as a session guitarist. It was at these *Hearts In
Danger* sessions (recorded at Chipping Norton and produced by Mike
Vernon) that Williams made the acquaintance of Jeff Rich (drummer) and
John 'Rhino' Edwards (bassist).

John 'Rhino' Edwards & Jeff Rich

John Victor Edwards was something of a violin prodigy as a young boy
(even securing himself a scholarship to the London College of Music) but
was drawn to rock and pop music after hearing the Beatles' debut single
'Love Me Do' when he was just ten years old. After switching to guitar
from violin for a short time, it was a live gig by the band Free at Richmond
Athletic Ground in 1969 that inspired Edwards to take up the bass guitar,
after being mesmerised by bassist Andy Fraser. Interestingly, he saw Quo
as a teenager at the Winning Post while they were promoting the 1971
album *Ma Kelly's Greasy Spoon* and became a casual fan of the band for a
short time.

Edwards' early professional credits include Nino Ferrer, Sandy Shaw, The Spamm Band and London prog-rock ensemble Rococo. His first taste of the UK singles charts, however came in the form of 'Magic Fly' – a number two hit for French synthpop band Space. He first met the bandleader Didier Marouani while recording with the Spamm Band in Paris, but not only is he largely uncredited for his playing on this cut, but all promotional footage has Edwards (and the rest of the band) disguised in ski suits and space helmets.

Soon after, guitarist (and future Quo producer) Mike Paxman recruited Edwards and Rich for Judie Tzuke's studio and touring band.

John Rhino Edwards in *Ultimate Guitar.com* in 2010:

> ...I was at a party and I knew [Mike Paxman] vaguely. They'd just got the money from Rocket Records that day to get a deal, and he'd seen me playing loads. We were both really shitfaced. And he said 'if you can remember my phone number and call me tomorrow, you've got the gig'. I've actually got a really brilliant memory for phone numbers...

Despite playing several albums backing the London-born singer-songwriter, the best representation of the quality of this band can be found on the 1982 live album *Road Noise*.

1982 was a busy year for the bassist; Edwards also managed to impress the popular UK act Dexy's Midnight Runners at an audition simply by tuning his bass with harmonics, and became their studio and touring bassist until 1985 and played on the *Don't Stand Me Down* album – a commercial flop at the time that has recently been reappraised as some of the band's best work.

By 1985, Edwards was often working with several acts at once and balancing a diary filled with studio and live dates that would soon become overwhelmed by Quo's comeback touring schedule.

Jeff Rich began playing drums at around age nine – initially inspired by Gene Krupa, Mitch Mitchell, John Bonham, Keith Moon and Kenny Jones. His first professional credits came with Stretch – a band featuring Kirby Gregory of Curved Air and singer Elmer Gantry. Their debut single 'Why Did You Do It' didn't feature Rich's drumming on the record (it was founding member Jim Russell) but many of the live and playback performances did. He worked as a studio and touring drummer for the band until 1978.

While maybe not quite as prolific as Edwards, Rich worked as a busy studio and touring musician for several acts before meeting Edwards in the Climax and Tzuke bands. Most interestingly, he started early with Jackie Lynton; friend and collaborator to Status Quo since the '70s.

Jeff Rich:

> I loved the Quo. In fact, I'd been with Jackie Lynton's band for a year or so, doing some gigs with him and Quo – they had the same management at the time. We did a gig together at the Kursaal in Southend-on-Sea [1 March 1975]. It was a wooden structure and when Quo played there, I remember thinking, 'this place is gonna fall down'... the whole place was shaking.
>
> We did our set first, and Francis came backstage to the dressing room and he said to Jackie, 'you don't wanna swap drummers do you? Your bloke is so much better than ours – you can have ours with pleasure'. When I eventually joined the band, he said to me 'I knew you'd join in the end! I always wanted you to be in the band, but the timing wasn't right'.

Edwards and Rich began working together in the Climax Blues Band also, and although no studio records were made during their time in the Climax Blues Band, an excellent concert from the Marquee Club was filmed in 1984. It shows Edwards at his funkiest and leaning on playing styles borrowed from Stanley Clarke and Jaco Pastorius.

As the pair had worked together extensively as part of Judie Tzuke's touring and studio band, it made sense to hire the pair, as they knew each other's style, strengths and weaknesses – and Williams had been so impressed with their synergy as a rhythm section that he asked them along to the Parfitt sessions to work with Vicki Brown, Stevie Lange, and Katie Kissoon on backing vocals, Martin Ditcham on percussion and Bias Boshell on keyboards.

Back at Chipping Norton, the *Recorded Delivery* sessions began. While the information regarding the tracklist is much more accessible than the one for *Flying Debris*, this is only because a low-quality bootleg has been doing the rounds online for many years and slightly amended versions of some tracks later appeared as Quo B-sides. There was a concerted effort from Pip and his assembled crack team of musos to make a modern-sounding stadium-rock record that could rival the efforts of Def Leppard, Bon Jovi and Van Halen while still representing Parfitt's cabaret roots and penchant for traditional and 60s-sounding melodies and lyrics.

Jeff Rich:

That was my first time playing with Rick. I'd met him a few times over the years but not on a friendly basis. I remember that he walked into the studio, played us the songs and we started rehearsing them and went from there. It was great fun – a great album to have worked on. There were some really good songs on there.

The most known (to Quo fans) of these songs came in the form of 'Halloween' – a Parfitt/Williams-penned track that features some suitably '80s guitar pyrotechnics from Williams and his tremolo arm. On the surface, the song's spooky overtones are cinematic, albeit light-hearted; but a closer 21st-century inspection of the lyrics could leave some concerned about the promiscuous predilections of the fictional character that Parfitt embodies here. The song was later released as a B-side to Quo's 1988 single 'Who Gets the Love' now with a third (although benign) writing credit afforded to Rossi for some additional guitar overdubs he provided before release. It was officially released a second time as the closing track to Parfitt's posthumous debut solo album *Over and Out* in 2018. While the track does not fit the rest of the album aesthetically, Parfitt wished for it to be included as a recording he was proud of – one that he felt had not reached its full potential as a largely unknown B-side.

'999 (One Good Reason)' had possible single potential if the recording had been mixed and mastered. A song written by Damon Danielson and Pat DeRemer that the composers were keen to see recorded and transformed into a hit record. It was later recorded by Puerto Rican boy band Menudo that (at the time) included a teenage Ricky Martin, although the band has gone through more line-up changes than almost any popular music ensemble, with over 30 performers being in the five-piece band at different times. '999' was recorded again, this time by Mari Hamada – a Japanese rock vocalist who included the song on her 1987 album *In the Precious Age*. The album is an obscure cut but features a band partially made up of brothers Mike and Jeff Pocaro. All three versions of the track (including Parfitt's) open with the same vocal delay effect before launching into a quasi-rock groove. Rhino provides some tasty bass playing here – on his Alembic bass as this was before he began endorsing Status Graphite instruments.

Totally unrelated to a similarly titled Quo B-side from 1974, 'Lonely Nights' stands out as one of the strongest cuts on the unreleased album.

While the composer has never been officially confirmed, it's probably a Parfitt-penned song with a synth-heavy pop groove complete with Parfitt's trademark lightly syncopated doublestop backing figures and a catchy refrain. There's a guitar and synth solo section that provides some 'rock' to the roll of the arrangement.

A cover of Neil Young's 'Only Love Can Break Your Heart' was also recorded for inclusion and Parfitt delivers a heartfelt, vulnerable vocal over the slow waltz that feels a little rhythmically stunted in places. Some pretty upper register fills from Rhino and two sublime solos from Williams, unfortunately, don't distract enough from the lack of swing from the overall performance.

'Don't Give It Up' is a masterclass in pop/rock production and performance and would have been a hit had it been given the chance. It's considered Rhino's first writing credit for a Quo-related project and was co-written with Canadian producer Richard Lightman. Rhino played it to Parfitt during the sessions and Parfitt liked it enough to add some bits of his own. When it was used as a B-side to 'Red Sky' in 1986, Rossi was added as a fourth composer and the royalties went on to be split four ways equally. The sound of the chorus-effected Alembic bass is crystal clear on both versions and features some of the bass player's best on record. The synthesised brass is later humiliated by a roaring tenor sax solo.

'Long Legged Girls' is another Parfitt/Williams track about what is appearing to be their favourite subject. It features another lyric that hasn't aged so well and thankfully wouldn't be judged favourably in the 21st century. Interesting that Parfitt again uses the acronym 'S.T.s' after its meaning initially eluded fans when used in 1976's 'Mystery Song'. It has since become common knowledge among fans that this refers to a woman's stocking tops. Once again, the bass guitar is doubled by a synth that seems to date the recording more than Williams probably planned. The backing vocalists are in full flight here and add an element of soul to proceedings. It was later used as a B-side to 'Dreamin' from November 1986.

'Show Me the Way' is a Parfitt/Williams track that is much more emotional than the preceding track. It was allegedly going to be dedicated, upon release, to the woman who would become Parfitt's wife, Patty. Patty Beeden had recently rekindled their friendship after moving back from Australia and selling her fashion business, and she was keen to support her old flame through his divorce and grief. A clean, Stratty-sounding guitar solo from Williams follows another growly and soulful tenor sax solo. Towards the end of the tracklist, we begin to see a more vulnerable Parfitt – a side of his

Above: Promotional picture c.1984 (l-r) Pete Kircher, Rick Parfitt, Alan Lancaster, Andrew Bown, Francis Rossi.

Below: Promotional picture c.1988 (l-r) John 'Rhino' Edwards, Andrew Bown, Rick Parfitt, Francis Rossi, Jeff Rich – featuring the uncharacteristic Charvel guitars.

Left: *Just Supposin'* from 1980. (*Vertigo*)

Right: The 'What You're Proposing' single cover. A number two U.K. hit in 1980. (*Vertigo*)

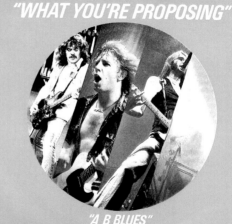

Left: A mimed performance of 'What You're Proposing' for Dutch T.V. show *TopPop*.

Right: *Never Too Late* from 1981. The last album to feature the Frantic Four. (*Vertigo*)

Left: A press advertisement for the 'Something 'Bout You Baby I Like' single release.

Right: A mimed performance of 'Something 'Bout You Baby I Like' for Dutch T.V. show *Bananas* – Bernie Frost stands in for Andy Bown and Lancaster is missing completely.

STATUS QUO
1982

Left: *1+9+8+2* from, of course, 1982. It was new drummer Peter Kircher's first with the band. (*Vertigo*)

$$= $$

Right: The 'Dear John' single cover from 1982. (*Vertigo*)

Left: The 'Ol' Rag Blues' single cover, a number 9 U.K. hit in 1983. (*Vertigo*)

Right: *Back to Back* from 1983. I was to feature four hit singles. (*Vertigo*)

Left: The 'Marguerita Time' single, was another massive hit in the U.K., reaching number three. (*Vertigo*)

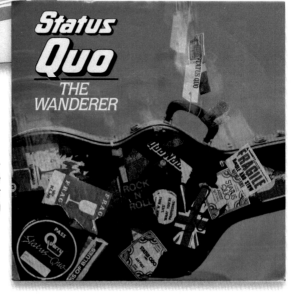

Right: 'The Wanderer': a stand-alone single of a song made famous by Dion. It was another top ten hit in the U.K. (*Vertigo*)

Left: Rossi playing 'What You're Proposing' for the Dutch T.V. show *TopPop*.

Right: Coughlan looks unengaged during the performance of 'What You're Proposing' for *TopPop*.

Left: The Frantic Four on *TopPop*.

Right: Live at the N.E.C. for the Prince's Trust 1982.

Left: Playing 'Roll Over Lay Down' as the crowd chants along.

Right: Rossi even pre-recorded the first six bars of the national anthem for the opening of the event.

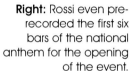

Left: A *Top of the Pops* promo appearance for 'Going Down Town Tonight' – on borrowed guitars!

Right: Lancaster claimed that the only member of the band on the track is Rossi!

Left: Kircher was a solid, no-frills drummer – the perfect side man and session player for Rossi.

Right: 'Going Down Town Tonight': Rossi was cajoled into the recording of the Guy Johnson song by the band's management.

Left: Lancaster at Milton Keynes Bowl on the End of the Road Tour.

Right: The show was a show of force by the band, treating the audience to both hits and album tracks.

Left: Opening Live Aid in July 1985.

Right: The band were allegedly mostly sober for their performance at Live Aid.

Left: Rossi claimed to have never seen as many T.V. cameras before or since.

Right: The band were under-rehearsed and took a few minutes to get their groove back

Left: 'Rocking All Over the World' became the unofficial anthem for the event.

Right: Like a few acts that played that day, Live Aid gave the band a new lease of commercial and creative life.

Left: *In the Army Now* from 1986, another top ten hit. *(Vertigo)*

Right: A new look for the 'Army' single promo video – with a new rhythm section.

Left: The 'In the Army Now' single. One of the Quo songs that has seeped into the public consciousness beyond that band's traditional fanbase. *(Vertigo)*

Status Quo
Ain't Complaining

Right: The *Ain't Complaining* album from 1988. *(Vertigo)*

Left: The run of hits continues with the 'Burning Bridges' single. *(Vertigo)*

Right: The 'Running all Over the World' single cover. The song – released for Sport Aid – was recorded in an afternoon. (Vertigo)

Left: The new line up returned to the N.E.C. to film another concert on the *Perfect Remedy* Tour 1989.

Right: Andrew Bown during the N.E.C. soundcheck.

Left: An animated John Rhino Edwards at the N.E.C.

Right: New drummer Jeff Rich, arrived at the same time as Edwards, both musicians having previously been in Judie Tzuke's band.

Left: A classic Quo pose during the N.E.C. concert.

Right: ... and they are then joined by Rhino Edwards.

Left: The *Perfect Remedy* album – the last of a turbulent decade. (*Vertigo*)

Right: The classic *12 Gold Bars* compilation released in 1980. (*Vertigo*)

Left: *12 Gold Bars Volume 2* released in 1984. It was in an effort to promote this album that Rossi and Parfitt agreed to perform on the Band Aid single 'Do They Know It's Christmas'. (*Vertigo*)

musical persona that Rossi would claim to miss in later years.

'Late Last Night' is a surprisingly rare composition from Rossi, Parfitt and Bob Young that dates back to the *If You Can't Stand the Heat* sessions but, while recorded as a basic demo, never saw the light of day until Parfitt suggested it for *Recorded Delivery*. This track sports an energetic, straight-ahead boogie groove with a guitar solo from Williams that is more Rossi-like than the man himself. It was used (without amendment) as a B-side to the 12" single of 'In the Army Now'.

'I Miss My Baby' is a Parfitt-penned track that is considered to be both a soulful outpouring of grief over the loss of his daughter Heidi and the separation from his wife Marietta. The true meaning is unknown, but either interpretation could be correct. The song is written in the diatonic style of the '50s and '60s pop songs that Parfitt frequently cited as his favourites. The final chorus is a struggle vocally, but the strained adlibs help to define the heartache of the song's lyrical content.

The closing song has been known by several titles – 'Living My Life Without You' and 'Richard's Song', but was eventually confirmed to be 'Without You'. The song was eventually rerecorded by Parfitt under the latter for his album *Over and Out*, released in 2018. There is no question that this lyric really is about the regret around the time spent away from his son Rick Parfitt Junior. The singer's failed marriage and the band's intense schedule had all but estranged him from his son. Thankfully, the father-son relationship was to be repaired and Parfitt Jnr. would go on to project manage his father's posthumous debut solo album release that features this very song, albeit with a thicker arrangement. While the original 80s recording features a plethora of synth layers and a suitably '80s guitar solo to boot, the 21st-century version boasts an augmented string quartet and a more organic piano backing.

Jeff Rich:

> Rick really liked our playing and he kept saying to us, 'you're much better than the guys we've got in [Quo]'. Then he told us that Alan Lancaster didn't want to come over to the UK to record with the band and that he wanted to make a record in Australia and there was a bit of a stand-off between them.

Parfitt went over his advance budget of £100,000 to make his solo album and even then, the record company was not impressed with the finished result, meaning he had to fund the extra costs himself.

Rick Parfitt in *Just For the Record:*

> They didn't recognise my voice. It was turned down flat… After my
> album was turned down, I thought, 'That's it. I've had it'… the taxman
> was after me for huge sums of money which I didn't have.

In fact, the heady mix of financial skulduggery from management and
lives of great excess from the band meant that Rossi and Parfitt ended up
making personal appearances in nightclubs to answer inane questions
from the public in order to make ends meet – Rossi (who was in a slightly
better situation than Parfitt) even took out a mortgage on his Purley home
The Glade.

Band Aid – Do They Know It's Christmas

Following a BBC report by Michael Buerk on 23 October 1984,
Boomtown Rat and out-of-vogue pop star Bob Geldof set about
correcting a miscarriage of human justice. The feature in question was
filmed in Ethiopia and depicted a 'biblical famine' that was so harrowing
that Geldof re-evaluated his feelings around the decline of his own
career to focus on making a difference to the less fortunate the only way
he knew how.

Purely by chance, he immediately called his then-partner Paula Yates,
who was backstage on *The Tube* – a British music magazine show she co-
presented. Also in the vicinity was Ultravox's Midge Ure and, when Geldof
became aware of this, he demanded Yates put him on the line. Ure was
soon recruited as co-composer and co-producer and gave Geldof's new
Christmas charity record project the legitimacy it required to involve the
other stars of the day.

Between them, Geldof and Ure swiftly recruited stars such as Phil
Collins, Sting, Bono, Paul Weller, Boy George, Paul Young, George Michael
and members of Spandau Ballet, Heaven 17, Duran Duran, Bananarama
and of course, Status Quo. On the morning of 25 November 1984, the
artists began arriving at Sarm West Studios in London.

The compilation album *12 Gold Bars Volume 2* had been released that
month, and manager Colin Johnson persuaded Rick and Francis to do it
as their inclusion in Band Aid may provide some second-hand exposure
for their own album.

Rossi, Parfitt and Bernie Frost (who simply came along for the fun of
it) arrived feeling decidedly out-of-place. If Geldof and the Rats were

out of fashion, Quo were ancient relics of the UK pop scene. Their career was literally over – the End of the Road tour had finished months before and there were no plans to get together for anything musical whatsoever. The two faces of the band were nervous to be around the big hitters of the day and were unsure of how they would be involved or even how they would be around each other after the split. Although Quo were friends with Sting and Phil Collins (and Rick knew Paul Weller after lending him an amplifier as a young upstart), their presence among the young blood was unsettling for them. Thankfully, Rick and Francis quickly got back to their old double-act antics like they had never been apart. They also took an uninitiated and nervous Paul Young under their wing, as he was as anxious as they were to be around the established stars. While Quo were the fossils of the scene, Young was freshly famous, and a little wet behind the ears.

While some of what they recorded was deemed unusable due to Parfitt's inability to pitch his harmonies properly (allegedly because of excessive cocaine and alcohol use on the day), some familiar dulcet tones can be heard quite clearly on the middle eight of the song (the 'here's to you…' line especially). Rossi ended up singing both harmonies on this section by doing a 'passable impression' of Parfitt – something he frequently did in the studio. If this is true, fans can rest easy knowing that Parfitt was present for the group chorus at the end of the track – he's on it, just not where you'd like to have heard him.

Spandau Ballet's Gary Kemp described Rick and Francis as the 'naughty schoolboys' of the day' and with good reason. The Quo boys reportedly had their own area of the green room named 'Rick and Franny's Fun Corner' where they benevolently shared their extensive selection of drugs and alcohol. These antics eventually resulted in Rick and Francis (now known by their new mullet-toting friends as 'The Doctors') locking Duran Duran in the toilets and repeatedly calling Phil Collins 'Joan', much to his chagrin.

Things got even more surreal when Nigel Planer turned up (uninvited) as Neil Pye – his character from *The Young Ones*. Remaining totally in character for his time at Sarm, he was eventually removed from the building by Geldof but not before he collared Quo outside the toilets and lent Parfitt his cheap acoustic guitar. Footage still exists of this strange encounter and Parfitt is quite clearly on another planet as he serenades the corridor with a chorus of 'Rockin' All Over the World'.

Rossi and Parfitt only appear in the official promo video at the end for the group refrain. Rossi is caught looking at Jody Watley's backside and

Rick natters away to Paul Young mid-chorus, but other than this, there's very little visual proof of their involvement.

Recorded, mixed and mastered in under 24 hours, the track became the fastest-selling single of all time until Elton John stole the accolade for himself with 'Candle in the Wind '97". It was released on 3 December 1984 and went straight in at number one. It went on to raise £8 million for the charity and put Status Quo back in the world spotlight – even if only for a few seconds.

1985: Live Aid and Lawsuits

Quo's contribution to the Band Aid single may have been minimal, but their participation in the follow-up concert Live Aid would prove to be legendary. The performance would last less than 13 minutes and yet it gave Quo their second chance – the hype surrounding their opening of the concert reinvigorated the public's love of the consistent, ubiquitous nature of Status Quo.

To all intents and purposes, Quo were the bottom of the bill (with the exception of the Coldstream Guards band). Quo weren't just 'not in the charts' anymore – they had broken up. The End Of The Road tour was a not-too-distant memory, but the band were barely even on speaking terms. Rossi, Parfitt and Lancaster were all working on different projects of their own and Bown had gone off to join Roger Waters' studio band for the concept album *The Pros and Cons of Hitch Hiking*. Drummer Pete Kircher had all but retired from music completely and was showing no real desire to return.

When Bob Geldof called to ask about the band taking part, Rossi outright refused claiming that the band wasn't just under-rehearsed but that it simply didn't exist anymore.

Alan Lancaster told Per Engelbo:

What happened was that Iain Jones said that Bob Geldof wanted us to open the show at Live Aid. I said 'great, I want to do it', but Iain told me that Francis didn't want to do it at this stage. Basically I said to Iain Jones 'tell Francis if he doesn't want to do it, I'll make sure everybody knows why we didn't do it'. Then it didn't take long before Iain came back and told me we were going to do Live Aid...

Parfitt, however, was very interested. He was grieving the loss of his band and the friendships it once had and was starting to believe that his own feelings and thoughts had not been listened to when the band had originally broken up. Geldof eventually browbeat Rossi into playing, allegedly claiming, 'it doesn't matter a fuck what you sound like, so long as you're there'. Rossi and Parfitt had been keeping themselves busy during Quo's hiatus – the former not just with his new project with Bernard Frost, but also making an impromptu one-song appearance with Dire Straits during their *Brothers in Arms* tour at Wembley Arena just days before Live Aid and a mere spitting distance from the latter's venue.

He joined them on guitar for album cut 'Two Young Lovers' – a Quo-style boogie track that would have gone down just as well at a Quo gig. The previous September, Parfitt had joined Queen for their encore at the same venue, delivering his signature driving boogie to their pacey version of 'Jailhouse Rock'.

Although the Quo had agreed to open the show as per the request of Mike Appleton (BBC producer and Live Aid programmer), a cynical Rossi was still unsure of Geldof's intentions and as a result, the band didn't rehearse at all until their soundcheck on the day before the show. Allegedly, Quo were the only act on the day to get a soundcheck due to the tight time frame the crew were working with.

John Coghlan:

> I think Alan said he wanted to get me back in for Live Aid, but of course, the phone didn't ring but that's another story… I watched it, though – I was in the Isle of Man where I was living at the time and it sounded alright…

Quo began to take the spot seriously when they became aware of not only the political and humanitarian significance of the event but how far and wide their performance would be beamed across the world as the opening act of the biggest concert in history. Quo even helped promote the show on television more than any other act – mainly because Geldof was still recruiting the stars he needed to fill the 16-hour programme. According to Parfitt's girlfriend Patty, Quo had also been asked to perform at the Philadelphia concert the way Phil Collins was scheduled to, but refused, thinking that it was best to not be upstaged by the American artists in a country that didn't much care for the British boogie-rockers anyway. If this is true, it could have been the cross-Atlantic exposure the band had always needed.

On 13 July, after meeting for drinks in Parfitt's local pub, The Raven in Battersea, Quo were eventually flown in over Wembley Stadium's 72,000-strong crowd to open the show. Rossi later claimed that he'd never seen so many TV cameras before or since and, for the first time since their early days as a band, began to feel some nerves.

After Tommy Vance announced their entry to the stage, Rossi walked up to the microphone to deliver his standard greeting 'How are you then, you alright!?' before launching into the signature tune of the event 'Rocking All Over the World'. While the broadcast mix (and the intonation of the vocal delivery) left a lot to be desired, the Quo magic was still making its presence felt. Both guitarists nail their guitar solos and the audience could not be any happier to hear this love-it-or-hate-it hit record played live at an event to change the world it claimed to rock all over.

Short on time, Parfitt promptly let rip into the opening riff of 'Caroline' before getting his right hand tangled up in an over keen cameraman's power cable. The rhythm didn't let up, though and the band felt a little more 'on form' as the song progressed – the vocals were stronger and the tempo was more appropriate for a live performance.

With time for one last number, Quo kicked off 'Don't Waste My Time' – a fan favourite album track from 1972 but not a song known by the wider public. After a humorous count-off by Rossi, the medium-tempo shuffle seemed to get Quo back on familiar ground and they now felt like a band that had never been away. Any nerves were gone, the rhythm was steady and tight and Rossi used Parfitt's exposed 8-bar rhythm guitar solo to get the entire crowd clapping in a spine-tingling unison nearly seven hours before Freddie did it with Queen.

Contrary to popular belief, Quo performed their set relatively sober. Once the band finished, Rossi retired to the makeshift Hard Rock Cafe backstage to hang with the likes of David Bowie and Queen and Parfitt flew back to a hero's welcome at his local public house. While Parfitt and his soon-to-be-wife Patty laid into the party atmosphere in Battersea, Rossi laid into the cocaine and tequila backstage in between being humorously manhandled by Freddie Mercury. By the time Rossi and Parfitt made their way back to the stage for their 'Feed the World' finale, both of them were so inebriated that they had no recollection of being there.

While Queen were largely considered to be the stealers of the show, it was Quo's performance that made the news over everybody else's. It set the tone for the event and championed the underdog efforts of both Geldof and Quo. The exposure the slot gave the band would be priceless – more so than any other public relations campaign or media coverage – and it proved to Rossi that there was still a market for Status Quo for at least the rest of the decade.

In 2005, Geldof launched another charity music project, 'Live 8' – a follow-up concert to Live Aid held in 10 countries (many simultaneously). Despite the band showing real desire to perform and several national newspapers calling for their inclusion with campaigns like 'No Show Without Quo' and 'The Quo Must Go On', they were denied a slot and their only representation on the day was Chris Martin of Coldplay rather tunelessly superimposing the 'Rocking All Over the World' chorus over their hit 'In My Place'. While the execution left many people bewildered, the thought was there.

Among the 1.9 billion watching the original concert through TV screens was Rhino Edwards and his wife Kathy, who were working a bar gig in Bermuda. Rhino pointed to Parfitt on the television and jokingly proclaimed, 'Hey! There's my new best mate!', not knowing the full extent of the truth he spoke.

The Gaslight Sessions

Sometime around the summer of 1985, Lancaster ventured into Gaslight Studios to lay down the basic ideas for his contributions to the new Status Quo album. While Lancaster maintained that Bown and Parfitt accompanied him to the sessions, the resulting bootleg recordings (released piecemeal through Lancaster's personal Facebook account around 2012) seem to be the work of Lancaster and several studio side-men with the finishing touches for several tracks being added in Australia. The bassist had taught himself to write and record in a much more commercial manner and undoubtedly wanted to make good on his promise to the fans regarding 'upping' Quo's writing and recording game but he would ultimately be denied the opportunity and seemingly lose his hard rock predilections in the process.

Francis Rossi in *Just for the Record:*

> Alan wanted to do a cheap album in Australia. He was convinced that we could do one for sixty grand. This was unlike him because he had always been a perfectionist about recording.

'One of a Kind' is a particularly commercial-sounding pop rock anthem that would have quite possibly been a hit for Quo had they recorded it. The song has several 'Quo-isms' that would have appealed to both sides of the ever-widening fan base – an anthemic chorus, emotionally charged harmonic movements and carefully considered guitar and tenor sax work that was both radio friendly and just raucous enough to please fans of the 'Whatever You Want' era. Written by Dave Skinner of Roxy Music with Lancaster, this track is probably the best of the bunch.

'That's All I Gotta Say' is a slow shuffle that could have easily been from the pen of Rossi and Frost – it's highly likely that Lancaster was trying to emulate the sound of the pair's compositions in order to gain thei. respect or approval as he felt more and more isolated from his colleagu Some of Lancaster's earliest influences are present here, with more raunchy double-tracked tenor sax providing a '50s rock 'n' roll 12/8 feel to the introduction, with the chord sequences later following suit. A live horn section completes the sound that Huey Lewis and the News would later rule supreme over the USA charts with.

'One Step Forward' is one of the weaker compositions represented here but one that would have been improved with a final recording and mixdown. Female backing vocals and more live horns provide sforzando pads but would have added to the overall effect in the hands of a producer like Pip Williams.

The most 'Quo'-like of all the demos is 'Put Your Money Where Your Mouth Is' – a straight-eight pub-rock track that would have fitted right onto *If You Can't Stand the Heat*. It features several of the sweetening elements of the previous tracks but is a bit more unapologetically rocky with its boogie riff and Chuck Berry-style licks. More raspy tenor sax adds a Springsteen-esque vibe to proceedings.

Rossi was reluctant to take part in Lancaster's venture for a number of reasons. He had little interest in making records on a tight budget and knew that if he should give in to the bassist's demands, it would set a dangerous precedent for future business decision-making. Most importantly, though, Rossi felt he could no longer work with Lancaster due to the chasmic creative differences that had slowly surfaced between the two founding members over the last ten years.

Lancaster allegedly tried to recruit Parfitt for 'Status Quo 2.0' and oust Rossi in the process due to the lead guitarist's reluctance to record or tour. Parfitt's financial dire straits almost forced him into taking the bait to form a new Status Quo that was more aligned with Lancaster's vision for the group, but Phonogram were not interested in a Status Quo without the green Telecaster-toting frontman. Parfitt supposedly hadn't the heart to tell Lancaster this while the bassist put plans in place to move his family back to the United Kingdom in order to make 'Quo Mk 2' work.

Partners In Crime & Diesel (1985)

Since leaving Quo, drummer John Coghlan had been busy with his own musical projects. His ad-hoc band Diesel was formed around 1976-1977 and featured a flexible line up of Coghlan, Bob Young, Andy Bown,

ordon Edwards of the Pretty Things, John Fiddler of
d Jackie Lynton – friend and occasional collaborator to
rly appearances were at the Marquee Club in Soho,
vived the band during 1985 to quench his thirst for

...n Coghlan

I put the Diesel band together – that was really good fun with Jack Lynton
and Mickey Moody. We never had to rehearse, we just got on with it. Bit
of blues… we all liked the blues. I wasn't the boss, though – it was so that
everybody could get together and play whatever they feel.

On 9 July 1985 (four days before Live Aid and one day after Rossi's
appearance with Dire Straits), Diesel played their seventh show of the year
on their home turf at the Marquee Club. The band at this time featured
Coghlan on drums, Lynton on vocals, Young on harmonica, Moody on
guitar, John Gustafson of Roxy Music on bass and Gothic Horizon's Mike
Simmons on keyboards. The encore, however, featured the surprise of
Parfitt and Lancaster joining the band for 'Caroline', 'Roadhouse Blues',
'Mess of Blues' and 'Bye Bye Johnny'. Parfitt had jumped up with Lemmy
of Motorhead on 4 April for 'Mess of Blues' which is probably what
inspired another appearance while Lancaster was in town in preparation
for the 13th.

Not one to rest on his laurels, Coghlan had also been working with
his new band, the Partners in Crime (originally named 'Freeway') – a
'supergroup' project featuring Noel McCalla of Moon as singer, Ray Major
of Mott on guitar, Mark de Vanchque of Wildfire on keyboards and Mac
McCaffery on bass. Coghlan had amassed a wealth of musical friends
since turning pro and was no stranger to these 'supergroups'. Alongside
Diesel, he had also contributed to a single release with 'The Rockers' – an
ensemble consisting of Phil Lynott, Chas Hodges and Roy Wood. The song
'We Are the Boys (Who Make All the Noise)' was a medley of old rock 'n'
roll numbers arranged by Wood. The record reached only number 81
on the UK singles chart, but the concept predated the success of similar
projects by Jive Bunny and even Quo's own 'Anniversary Waltz' in 1990.

With the Partners in Crime, a single, 'Hold On' – a Yes song from 1983
written by Chris Squire, Trevor Rabin and Jon Anderson – was released
to a modicum of critical acclaim but, unfortunately, was to set a low
commercial standard for their following releases. A complete album (that

also featured all the band's past and future A and B-sides) was produced by John Eden and released in 1985. *Organised Crime* was put out by the Epic label to significant interest from DJs and critics. It sported a slick soft-rock production and solidly composed material that was akin to that of Def Leppard, Foreigner and Toto and can be considered to be among some of Eden's best production work during the 1980s. Sadly, it was not to be; after the commercial failure of the album and its preceding and succeeding singles, the band broke up, leaving a bitter taste in Coghlan's mouth, who felt like the project deserved a bigger and better reception from the public who were evidently a little tired of the new, but ubiquitous commercial album-oriented-rock sound.

John Coghlan:

> The management wasn't very good and the record company didn't really push it and I think it could have been better. The album was great and it was recorded well – Noel McCalla had a wonderful voice. It's a shame, it could have been good, it could have been a famous band… if we'd pushed it a little more… –

At the time of writing, the recorded output of the band has only ever been released on vinyl format, and the handful of live shows the band performed (five in total, all in London over 1984 & 1985) are hard to find any record of. One at the Paris Theatre in January 1985 was recorded and broadcast by the BBC but has still yet to see an official release.

Lawsuit

To say Lancaster's dismissal from Status Quo was acrimonious would be something of a grave understatement, but in fact, to call it a dismissal is inaccurate – he was simply left out of any further Quo projects.

By the time Francis and Rick had begun work on what was to become *In The Army Now*, Lancaster was unaware that anything was even happening in the Quo camp. Although he'd been devastated at the loss of his band, he'd accepted the end had come and began to sink his energy into other projects in his adopted homeland of Australia.

By 1985, Alan had been told via several (unnamed but reliable) sources that Status Quo had studio time booked at Chipping Norton and he began questioning this with Quo's management company Quarry, who vehemently denied the accusation that Rossi and Parfitt were continuing

Status Quo without him. Several faxes detailing this correspondence were leaked online in 2016 but were soon removed. Lancaster also believed that his final financial cut from the End of the Road Tour had been grossly under-calculated and was also interested in rectifying this. While Francis and Rick were unaware of the full scale of the band's financial situation at the time, they would, in later years, go on to back up Lancaster's claims that someone in the management was conning the band out of millions of pounds from both their touring income and their estimated 120 million record sales.

Alan Lancaster in a Studio 10 TV interview:

> We'd had more hits than any other band in the world, but we didn't sell as many copies... From my royalty statements, it's around 35 to 40 million. None of us in the band have ever received a royalties statement ever. We've never had an accounting from management. There's lots of millionaires going around the world who've made their money from Status Quo, but the band themselves, they struggled to get theirs.

In truth, it was Rossi and Parfitt that the record company knew would sell records as the faces of Status Quo – not Lancaster. As a result, Phonogram were happy to let the guitarists fulfil their contractual obligations on the proviso that Rossi's wishes to be creatively separated from Lancaster were adhered to. While Lancaster wasn't fired as such, the ultimatum Francis gave the record company meant that they had to pick either him or Lancaster to continue Status Quo and they went wholeheartedly with the established frontman of over 20 years.

Feeling betrayed, Lancaster took Rossi and Parfitt to court to prevent them from recording or touring under the name of Status Quo, which would ultimately be a financial mistake for the bassist. Lancaster's injunction prevented the 'Naughty Girl' single (which eventually became 'Dreamin'') from releasing on time but ultimately led to the courts ruling in favour of Rossi and Parfitt, apparently much to Lancaster's fury. The bassist later claimed that the feeling of being sacked from his band was akin to having his 'child abducted'.

Alan Lancaster speaking to *Classic Rock* Magazine in October 2016:

> Status Quo ended up costing me more money than I ever made from it because I was trying to protect it. I'm not a big corporation any more, I'm on my own. In the end, you have to give up.

He eventually accepted his fate as an ex-member of Status Quo and wouldn't join them in a creative capacity again until 2012 when he began rehearsals for the much anticipated 'Frantic Four' reunion shows with Coghlan reprising his role on the drum stool.

1986: In the Army Now

In The Army Now

Personnel:

Francis Rossi: guitar, vocals

Rick Parfitt: guitar, vocals

John 'Rhino' Edwards: bass guitar, vocals

Jeff Rich: drums

Andy Bown: keyboards, backing vocals

Additional musicians:

Paul 'Wix' Wickens: keyboards (uncredited)

Produced by Pip Williams, Dave Edmunds

Record Label: Vertigo

Recorded: Chipping Norton Studios and Jacobs Studios, Sept 1985- Feb 1986

Release date: 29 August 1986

Highest UK chart place: 7

Running time: 47:13

Side one: 'Rollin' Home' (John David) – 4:26, 'Calling' (Francis Rossi, Bernie Frost) – 4:04, 'In Your Eyes' (Francis Rossi, Bernie Frost) – 5:08, 'Save Me' (Francis Rossi, Rick Parfitt) – 4:25, 'In the Army Now' (Rob Bolland, Ferdi Bolland) – 4:41

Side two: 'Dreamin'' (Francis Rossi, Bernie Frost) – 2:55, 'End of the Line' (Ricky Patrick, Rick Parfitt) – 4:59, 'Invitation' (Francis Rossi, Bob Young) – 3:16, 'Red Sky' (John David) – 4:14, 'Speechless' (Ian Hunter) – 3:41, 'Overdose' (Pip Williams, Rick Parfitt) – 5:25

It was a bitter pill to swallow, but Rossi and Parfitt had to acknowledge the fact that, as talented as they may be as individuals, the record-buying public had little to no interest in either of them as solo entities. To make matters worse, both guitarists were in dire financial straits, and still owed Phonogram at least one more studio album under the name 'Status Quo'. After his success with the last Quo hit, 'The Wanderer', producer Pip Williams was brought back in at the behest of manager Colin Johnson who was still trying everything in his power to get Quo to crack America.

Francis Rossi:

[Williams is] a brilliant man – I learned a lot from Pip... of what to do and not to do. I used to call him 'nitpicker'... however, his nitpicking did produce really good vocal tracks that were pristine. From Pip, I learned how to format the record and mess with the arrangements and such.

That said, sometimes, 'musical ideas' [suggested by] musicians can become dangerous for chart success I think. When the musicianship in the band begins to take over... a lot of that gets lost on the general punters anyway... I think there's a fine line between where I want to be – ultimate commerciality – and real, pure musicianship.

Upon Parfitt and Williams' recommendation, Rossi was eventually cajoled into trying out the new rhythm section they had been working with. Although they weren't formally auditioned by Francis, the guitarists met with them at Gaslight Studios and Francis was characteristically polite but prickly in equal measure, with no real optimism regarding the rehearsal's outcome. By the end of the session, Francis expressed a new-found hope in the band and agreed with Parfitt that these younger session musicians would be the right fit for a new era of Status Quo.

Jeff Rich:

 Francis walked in and he wasn't a happy bunny – he hated change, even with things like setlists. He wouldn't want to put new songs in the set and would rather do the same things every time and usually in the same order. We started playing because we knew the songs anyway and they weren't difficult to learn. He was scowling around during the first number and then, all of a sudden, he looks up and his head's nodding. I could see him thinking, 'fuck me, this is great!' and by the end of the session, that was it. He thanked us and we were in the band.

A collateral victim of these new signings would be the career of drummer Pete Kircher. Although he was not officially fired from the band, it was clear that Edwards and Rich came as a pair and so the previous drummer's services were sadly no longer required.

Jeff Rich:

I always equate it to football. Quo would be in the Premier League, and my other pro bands like the Climax Blues Band, were in the Championship, so it was a big step up. Having said that, it didn't faze us in the slightest doing it – it was just a case of getting on with the job.

Although Rossi would later admit that he felt bad letting Kircher go this way, Kircher was already done with show business and by 1986 had happily returned to his old trade of sign writing. Kircher has since become something of a recluse and rarely participates in anything Quo or even music-related.

John Rhino Edwards:

> When Jeff and I got in, there was a move towards becoming an AOR band. With *In the Army*, there was quite a lot of thought towards [cracking] America on that one. When we cut that album, I wasn't in the band – it was just another project; another session job... Literally, the night I finished recording the album, I got driven to Hatfield to do the last production rehearsal before Judie Tzuke's tour started the next day. In fact, at the first proper TV show we did with Quo in Germany, I was on with Kim Wilde at 3 pm and Quo at 6 pm. I was still really busy as a session player. The phone used to ring in those days!

Not to be confused with 'Rolling Home' (Rossi/Lancaster) from 1976's *Blue For You*, 'Rollin' Home' gave Status Quo their post-break-up comeback single at number nine courtesy of Love Sculpture's John David. The record was released as a special edition 'Q' shaped picture disc. John David's bandmate Dave Edmunds was brought in to produce the track.

John Rhino Edwards:

> Dave Edmunds' production style was completely different to Francis' or Pip's. He came in, knew the song and knew exactly what he wanted.

It became the first of many collaborations between Quo and John David and makes regular appearances as part of the live set in the 'Mystery Medley'. It was also re-recorded for the *Aquostic* project in 2014. It's a mid-tempo rocker in the key of B major with the standard three primary chords, but the melody is catchy enough to carry the recording through. There's very little in the way of lead guitar breaks, and the ones that are present are doubled by the synths leaving the two guitarists to drive the track in Quo's traditional boogie style. Rather untraditionally for Quo, Rhino Edwards is not only playing bass guitar here but also a synth bass – a common production feature of 1980s pop music. Listen closely and you can hear the staccato attack of the keyboard bass. The video was recorded while on tour in the Middle East and features live footage mixed with film of the band engaging in their infamous dry, slapstick wit that foreshadows their *Bula Quo* movie excursion 27 years later. The film also documents Parfitt's first time in a swimming pool since the loss of his daughter. The single was backed with 'Lonely' – a shuffle track that grooves in a slinky way that no other track from this era of Quo's output does. Composers Parfitt and Rossi sing joint lead throughout, with the former on the higher voice and mixed above Rossi's lower part. The 12" release featured 'Keep Me Guessing' – a song dating back to the late '70s written by Bob Young, Rossi and Parfitt. It was originally intended to be recorded for the *If You Can't Stand the Heat* sessions but wasn't finished for reasons unknown. It features Parfitt in the lead vocal role with the harmonies overdubbed by Parfitt himself. It's an effective delivery of one of Parfitt's harder vocals that's paired with a roaring tenor sax solo.

Off of the strength of the single release in May and their previous associations with the charity, Rossi and Parfitt were invited to join the 'All-Stars' band (made up of the likes of Mark Knopfler, Mark King, Elton John, Bryan Adams, Phil Collins, Eric Clapton and musical director Midge Ure) at the Prince's Trust 10th Anniversary Rock Gala in June. While the other three members of Quo are absent from the show, the duo performed the last few numbers of the show as part of the backing band for Paul McCartney on songs like 'Saw Her Standing There', 'Long Tall Sally' and 'Get Back' – the latter of which also featured soul legend Tina Turner. The penultimate song of the evening was an impromptu strum through of 'Dancing in the Street' with the All-Star Band (with McCartney) backing Mick Jagger and David Bowie, but this recording is rarely featured on official releases of the concert attended by Princes Charles and Lady Diana.

'Calling' is an upbeat cut courtesy of Rossi and long-time collaborator Bernie Frost for an obvious second track for the album; a head-bobbing shuffle featuring several borrowed chords that are not native to the established key and as a result, the track was compared to fan favourite 'Don't Waste My Time'. While the synthesised licks haven't dated maybe as well as the band would have liked, the piano interjections perfectly complement the vocal throughout the verses. The overdubbed drum fills, such as the one after the first verse, are perfectly phrased triplets that echo the lyrical content of the chorus and previous track.

Jeff Rich:

There were hardly any drum machines in the studio by the time I was with them. One or two tracks may be a mix of live drums and sequenced drums, but never just the machine – it was used more for percussion… Sampling was just happening at that stage, so we were experimenting with snare sounds using triggers. We had a library of snare drum sounds triggered from one snare – whatever suited the track.

The guitar solo at 2:57 is among Rossi's best on the album and the legato lines are not rushed but phrased perfectly behind the beat.

'In Your Eyes' is another catchy album track from the Rossi/Frost camp written about Rossi's then-girlfriend Paige Taylor, that features a synthesised panpipe-type patch that at the time was enough to put some of the fans off the album for good. More than making up for this small oversight is the fantastic bass playing of then-new recruit John 'Rhino' Edwards, who begins to shine from this track onwards. He steps out with some conservative but effective lines to link the chord changes – most audible at places such as 1:09 and 1:44. During the guitar solo playout, there is a brief quote of Francis' 'Rocking All Over the World' solo at 4:47 that sounds too deliberate to be an accident or lack of musical imagination. It's especially hard to miss as the track is even in the same key of C major as the 1977 hit. It's a fun little Easter egg that was almost definitely kept in the mix at the behest of producer Pip Williams.

Francis Rossi

The solo was like a ship going down – the melody sounds like a naval thing. I imagine a guy standing on a ship saluting as the ship goes down.

One of a few rare compositional collaborations between the two frontmen, 'Save Me' is driven by a riff using similar triadic shapes that all members of the band have been known to use on countless other cuts like 'Whatever You Want', 'Hold You Back' and 'Liberty Lane'. It's a shuffle that pounds along with new rhythm section Rich and Edwards in perfect synchronicity. The outro solo is a composed line that is repeated to form another melodic hook. Rhino again peeps in and out with simple but effective low-end material.

'In The Army Now' is a brooding cut in D minor that was originally a hit for Dutch brothers Bolland & Bolland in 1982. Rossi had wanted to record a version for several years beforehand and now had carte blanche to do so with the internal politics in the band now firmly in his favour. It's a real departure for the band, but their version released in September 1986 gave the band a massive number two hit in the UK and several number ones around the world in countries such as Austria, Poland, Iceland and West Germany. The single's success in these territories is often attributed to the conscription laws and martial experiences of the people living in such places.

John Rhino Edwards:

I know Francis had found the song and I think Nuff [Lancaster] didn't want to do it, but Francis knew it was a huge song. With me and Jeff coming along, we were hardly gonna say 'no, we don't wanna do that' were we?… There had been some dismay in the band about how well records hadn't been selling – probably because so many fans had felt alienated by the change in material and so we were trying to diversify the band – away from the 'macho' image. We were trying to be radio-friendly.

Jeff Rich, talking to *Metalville.co.uk* in 2015:

…when you're in the studio a lot of the time you don't play the song as a band; you put a backing track down. So it would just be bass and drums and then everything's built around that. I mean, 'In The Army Now' was just literally… I think I put the kit down first and the bass went on separately. Everything went on separately. The whole track was built up and you don't know what it's going to sound like until you actually hear it at the end. You are always hearing bits of a track until it's mixed and then think, 'Oh, that's really good. I like that', or it might be a disappointment. You might think it's lost the essence of what the track was about to start with. I can't think of a specific track because of the way the band used to record. It wasn't like the old days where you'd go in, set everything up in a studio altogether and just record. The problem nowadays is you need separation. You can't get separation like that because everything spills into the mics. You can't, really. If someone makes a mistake and plays the wrong chord, it would go down all the other mics. You can't do that because you'd be forever trying to get down and everyone playing absolutely perfectly. Especially if they don't know the number properly – a new song.

There's a great big fat bass sound from Rhino here as he plays the 'Another Brick in the Wall'-type line featured on the original Bolland brothers recording. His entry at 0:49 is an inspired little flourish that introduces his simple root and 5th groove nicely. The drum break at 1:40 leads us to the new key of E minor and something of a mystery at 2:08 – the famous 'stand up and fight!' lyric. For many years it was reported that Slade's

Noddy Holder delivered the line (a rumour fuelled by an incorrect *Top of the Pops* caption), but it is generally believed to be either Chris 'Nut' Hatch or Mick Hardgrave – members of the band's crew. The guitar solo at 2:56 is simple and effective but stylistically unlike Rossi, which means that it was likely played (or at least composed) by producer Pip Williams – himself an accomplished guitarist and arranger. The video (mostly in black and white) saw the band in uncharacteristic, static, moody poses cut with dramatised colour footage of recruits in training. There was clearly an attempt to update the band's image here – a theory bolstered by the appearance of Andrew Bown with spiky hair and a keytar.

John Rhino Edwards talking to *Ultimate Guitar.com* in 2010:

> Well, at first, I felt like such a tw*t, it's no surprise people were gobbing at me. I mean, I look like a sort of... 12 inch mix of a Duran Duran song, you know. The first record I played [on] was 'In The Army Now', and the whole thing was 'we're changing the band – we're gonna change the style of the band'. For that side of it, I fitted in quite well. I had what you might call the 'pop image' of the time... I think we all got it wrong for a while. I think the band lost its way for a while, after the success of 'Army' and 'Burning Bridges'. It was going well, and then I think it went up its own arse a bit. It took me a good 15 years to slot in properly, I think.

It was backed with 'Heartburn' – a Parfitt track written with Sweet Sensation's Recardo Patrick that also credited Rossi as a third (but superficial) composer. Rossi's overall contribution to the released recording seems quite minimal – it sounds as if the guitar work is almost all Pip Williams and Parfitt, with the only evidence of Rossi's involvement in the group backing vocals. A 12" release also saw Parfitt's tune 'Late Last Night' included in the tracklisting. 'In The Army Now' was re-recorded and released in 2010 for charities 'Help for Heroes' and the 'British Forces Foundation'. Again produced by Pip Williams, this recording peaked at number 31 despite positive reactions to the new (and slightly less bleak) version from critics and fans. A promotional video filmed at Bulford Barracks in Wiltshire was directed by John Keeling. The song has featured in the live set on and off since its release and still gets occasional airplay on several '80s/rock radio stations.

Rumoured to be the first song written by the Rossi & Frost partnership in the early '70s, the up-tempo rock track 'Dreamin'' was originally titled 'Naughty Girl' and is available to hear in several different mixes. The song was used as the fourth and final single from *ITAN* in November 1986. It was played live occasionally on the '86 tour but has not been heard live since. The instrumental hook of the song is played by a synthesised horn section – in hindsight, these riffs and melodies would have benefited greatly from a real horn section being layered on top. The most obvious place that each mix differs is the breakdown starting before the modulation at around 1:32. While the album version features guitars riffing around in the major pentatonic with the synth providing broken chords on top, the single mix buries these elements and allows the rhythm guitars to take centre stage with a syncopated, heavily effected backing figure. The 'wet mix' that backed the extended 12" single features none of these elements and just chugs along with a simplified rhythm part. The song was supposed to be released under its original title as the comeback single (instead of 'Rollin' Home'), but Lancaster's lawsuit resulted in the 'Naughty Girl' mix being pulled. This initial mix is different again – Rick Parfitt can be heard improvising a vocal figure at around the 2:10 mark. By the time this song was eventually released on the album and later single, these vocal parts had been removed. It's undeniably catchy and features slick performances from every member of the band, but the choice of keyboard sounds have done much to dim its appeal to the hard-core fanbase. The video featured a light-hearted playback performance cut with footage of a plethora of extras, including dancing girls and a gorilla. The single made it to number 15 on the UK singles charts in winter 1986 and was backed with 'Long Legged Girls' from Parfitt's solo sessions.

'End of the Line' is probably the hardest rocking track on the album and is the second Parfitt-penned track written with Recardo Patrick. It's a memorable performance of a challengingly high vocal right at the top of Parfitt's chest voice range and certain moments of strained tuning add to the rough and ready delivery of the vocal. The composition makes good use of the Dorian mode and a pedalled bass note where the harmony moves around above it. The mix suffers from a distinct lack of Rhino's bass, but a few upper-register licks pop out here and there. There are some really nice backing vocal spreads throughout this track – something this line-up of the band did extremely effectively under the supervision of Pip Williams. The half-time breakdown at 2:53 exposes a synth bass doubling Rhino's part before leading to a section crying out for a screaming solo, although we're not treated to one until the fade-out.

'Invitation' is the first real surprise on the album, appearing on side two with this unapologetically country rock aesthetic. It's a Rossi/Young composition with a pretty melody and a motoring rhythm section. It was almost certainly written several years before when the songwriting duo were collaborating more regularly. There's definitely more than the standard three chords here and they provide a beautiful backdrop for Rossi and Parfitt to harmonise in the classic Quo two-part fashion with what sounds like Rossi adding a third harmony to the mix in places. The pedal steel-type guitar licks in the verses are almost certainly played by Pip Williams on what sounds suspiciously like a Stratocaster, whereas the slightly more driven lead parts appear to be provided by Francis on his Telecaster. While it could be argued that the song struggles to sit with the other rockier tracks on the album, the execution of the recording is hard to find fault with from a performance or production perspective.

'Red Sky' was a modest hit despite placing slightly below the other single offerings from the album and was another John David-penned composition in C minor and the second single released by the new line up. Dave Edmunds was again at the production helm and his style blends seamlessly with that of Pip Williams. Whether this was a conscious decision is unknown, but it is most likely a happy accident. Rossi and Parfitt seem to be attracted to the catchier cuts of David's portfolio of songs and the chorus of this one solidifies this theory. Even catchier than the chorus, though, is the main riff based on perfect fourths and the minor pentatonic scale in the style of ZZ Top. Rhino is again playing synth bass here – completely leaving the bass guitar out of the arrangement. Parfitt's harmonies are mixed nice and high for the choruses, which is a rare but welcome feature of the mix. Rossi's guitar solo at 2:22 waffles a little in places but builds to a very nice crescendo before tailing off with a frantic whammy bar dip or two. The single peaked at number 19 on the UK singles chart despite no official promo video ever seeing the light of day. It was released with 'Don't Give It Up' on the B-side – a cut originally slated for Parfitt's *Recorded Delivery*. Small Faces drummer Kenny Jones filled in for Jeff Rich on *Top of the Pops* while Rich was helping Def Leppard's drummer Rick Allen get through his band's tour after he lost an arm in a car accident.

Originally an album track on Ian Hunter's 1983 release *All the Good Ones are Taken*, the quirky cover version of 'Speechless' is everything you wouldn't expect from Status Quo, although it's a definite improvement on the original with a fatter arrangement and production. Allegedly written about the dangers of television, the song contains several interesting harmonic moments with ear-grabbing diminished chords and semitone movement. Rossi's delivery of the vocal may not be to everyone's taste, but there is a certain charm to his phrasing that can raise a smile on the casual listener's face. The trademark Quo harmonies are not really present, leaving Rossi's double-tracked vocal spending most of the time in its own wilderness. There's not much in the way of driving guitars or rocking bass here either, despite effectively arranged parts for everyone involved. Instead, the majority of the foreground is given to layered synthesisers and programmed elements.

The album's closer 'Overdose' could not have been better chosen, written or played. 'Overdose' has it all – the half-time verses, an earworm of a chorus and a fade-out that gives Rhino a playground of space to fill in his own unique way – he even suggested several drum fills to Rich.

Jeff Rich:

> The old Quo used to spend ages in the studio, but we helped speed the process up by having worked together loads before. We'd have what we'd call a pre-studio rehearsal to go through all the songs and so by the time we got them to the studio, they were done and dusted arrangement-wise and once we had a solid backing track, they could start putting the guitars on. Me and Rhino used to work our parts out together. Rhino's a frustrated drummer anyway – most bass players are! We'd suggest ideas to each other.

Dedicated to the memory of London nightclub owner Mark Raymond, this track from the pen of Rick and producer Pip, begins with the trademark inverted triads. The chord movements are common to both Quo and Pip Williams. After a short riff in the relative key of A minor, the first verse tonality shifts to A major through a series of major triads chromatically moving down over an A bass note. The chorus pops in at 2:12. It's a long time to wait, but it's worth it – the chorus and its preceding pre-chorus is catchy and well delivered by Parfitt. His lead vocal remains un-harmonised (but certainly double-tracked) until the first chorus, where we're greeted with a wonderful introduction to the sublime backing vocals doubling Rick in 3-part harmony. The backing vocals build throughout the track and help with the crescendo over the fade-out. When the intro riff appears again at 3:47, we're treated to Parfitt's ad lib vocals back in the key of C with little to no preparation. If you listen carefully enough, Rhino steals the show here with some of his most sublime playing on record.

John Rhino Edwards:

> Yeah, I quite like the bass playing on that. I did two fuck-off licks at the end of that track. Quite groovy, isn't it? When me and Jeff were working out the verse bits, I thought it was a bit 'Yes' actually – I thought it was a bit 'prog'. I came up with that drum fill before 'If I hold myself together…' – I told him to play that. One of the great things about Jeff, he never minded if I suggested anything. He's not much of a technician, though – there's a few things he can't do because he plays with his heel in the air… he used to really struggle at the end of 'Rocking all Over the World'.

Jeff Rich:

> Really, what we brought to the band was energy. Before we met them, we'd watched some footage of their last tour, and they were lame… no energy, going through the motions and I thought, 'this is not right – they're not putting anything into it'. When we played with them, we gave them a kick up the arse and that's what they liked about the whole thing. We were young… keen… I'd already taught myself to play a proper blues shuffle for the Climax Blues Band…

Among recent reissues of the album, a curiosity by the name of 'Rock 'n' Roll Floorboards' has made itself known, but with little to no information regarding its composition. Any listener au fait with popular music will instantly spot the shameless resemblance to Ike and Tina Turner's 'Nutbush City Limits', which is largely considered the reason for the song never being officially released (or even completely mixed) at the time.

John Rhino Edwards

> That was during the *Army* sessions, but we just aborted it. It wasn't happening.

The track has been credited at different times to Parfitt & Williams and Rossi & Frost, although neither writing team were responsible for the creation. The song actually came from Brian Alterman (of Kircher's band Shanghai), who recorded the demo in 1979. The Alterman cassette demo was given to Rossi by Kircher, who suggested it for the next Quo album. It is rumoured that it was one of the first two songs cut for the *Army* album along with 'Dreamin''.

In a 1994 *Keyboard Review* interview with Mark Cunningham, Bown mused on the album:

> Technically the best album we've ever made has to be *In the Army Now*, and it's generally a great mixture too. That had 'hit' written all over it… [Paul] 'Wix' Wickens played all of the brass sounds on it because I'm not a great synthesiser fan. What a lovely, clever geezer!

This is interesting as, although Wickens played on the *Recorded Delivery* sessions, he was never credited as a musician on a Quo record until 1988's *Ain't Complaining*.

Francis Rossi:

> I loved him [Wickens]. When the [Yamaha] DX7 [keyboard] first came out, he would go around doing demos for them, so he had the ultimate rig. He also had this funny thing you stuck in your gob for the sax or trumpet sounds, so it made the samples sound more kosher and he was really, really, really well-versed in that. I really thought of getting him in with us and having him as well [alongside Bown], but he was phenomenally expensive – he was always out with McCartney at the time but a delightful bloke… I'm not sure if Rick engineered this, but there was talk of leaving Andrew Bown out of the *Army* sessions. There was always a thing against Andrew Bown when I first wanted him in 1972 or '73. The band was always a five-piece – it always had a keyboard, but the Quo punters don't like the fucking keyboards. It always seemed to me that keyboards was the one area that could branch us out – to do anything. You could have brass, fiddles, anything you fucking want! It meant we could broaden what Status Quo were doing.

The album was the comeback record they had hoped for and notable for a complete lack of backing vocals from Bernie Frost – possibly at the recommendation of Rossi, Williams, Phonogram or maybe all three to ensure the Quo brand was not confused with the Rossi & Frost project. Released in August '86, it peaked at number seven on the UK album charts and was a commercial success – despite some fans criticising the attempt to modernise the sound of the band.

Rick Parfitt in *Classic Rock Magazine* in March 2017:

> The title song was great, but it had too many fillers.

Reviews were mostly fair to middling. Roger Holland's three-star review in *Sounds* seems to sum up the feelings of the public and a portion of the remaining fanbase at the time:

> Obviously, there's nothing here to rival the simple rock piledriver mentality of the prime-time 'Down Down', 'Rain' or 'Mystery Song', but then that isn't the game anymore. Over a generously long album, the new-look and confident Status Quo explore a variety of feels and styles. This band has, finally matured. And as long as you're prepared to part with the icon that has shaped all those long hours of mindless boogie, this is good news.

Before the album was released, Rossi was more interested in road-testing the new rhythm section of Rhino Edwards and Jeff Rich rather than the new material. The first shows took place in the United Arab Emirates in April 1986 and what became the 'Quo's Back Summer Tour' featured only classic Quo live staples to reel in punters and put the new boys through their paces. Quo were soon invited to join their friends, Queen, on their 'Magic Tour' of the same year, who were themselves enjoying a resurgence of interest since their immortal appearance at Live Aid. During the middle of their own tour, Quo opened all of Queen's UK stadium dates, starting at St. James' Park in Newcastle on 9 July and ending with the five-show run at Knebworth on 9 August – also Queen's last ever show with Mercury as frontman. Allegedly, Quo ended up firing a member of the road crew at this show due to him making his way to the top of the stage set and playing a cardboard guitar and getting a laugh from the audience during their set. While there is evidence to prove this happened, there is none to suggest that Quo actually sacked the roadie, but this day is notable for Quo for another reason.

Long before Quo set the world record for playing four shows in four different cities in less than 12 hours in 1991, they played three shows in three different countries in 24 hours – Denmark's Skandeborg Festival, Knebworth with Queen and Switzerland's Seepark Festival rounding off the short blast of appearances. Edwards apparently asked Rossi during the tour, 'so are we in the band or not!?' to which Rossi responded with nothing but praise for the bassist claiming he was 'in from the beginning' but that his drummer friend was the one they were truly road-testing. Nevertheless, Rich soon made the right impression and ended up as a full-time member of the band up until his departure in 2000.

Just under two months later, the tour morphed into the 'In the Army' tour – a behemoth world tour of 100 dates (inclusive of a warm-up show in Swindon at Faringdon Road Park). UK metal band Waysted opened Quo's UK shows, and the setlist included new tracks like 'Dreamin'', 'In the Army Now' and occasionally 'Save Me' and 'Overdose' on some early dates. Their Christmas eve show at the Hammersmith Odeon in London even featured Bob Young and Lemmy Kilmister for the 'Bye Bye Johnny' encore.

The fans weren't as welcoming to the new rhythm section as the band had hoped. Rhino Edwards was victim to heckling and even being spat at by fans who were furious that he'd taken Lancaster's position in the band. This was not ameliorated by the appearance of the punky, new-wave, trendy aesthetic of the bass player – used to *Top of the Pops* and *MTV* music videos.

John Rhino Edwards in *Ultimate Guitar:*

Yeah, I just want Nuff to understand that I'm trying to keep his legacy in a safe pair of hands. You know, I don't wanna fuck it up, they made some amazing records – they made some shit ones as well, let's be honest.

Rich remained largely unscathed from behind his kit but soon caught flak for racing through the older numbers at rapid tempos.

Jeff Rich:

When we started playing as a unit, the problem [with the tempos] was with Francis' and Rick's cocaine habit – everything was being pushed… I count in at one tempo, and all of a sudden, they'd be gone [to a faster tempo]! I was being blamed – normally by people who don't know shit about music – for playing too fast. The worst thing I could have done is to try and pull Francis and Rick back [rhythmically]. We just had to keep up because the [lack of] timing would be so noticeable otherwise. Drummers should be able to play in time, yes, but every musician in the band is responsible for tempo, timing and feel. You have to play as a unit. They were so coked up, they never noticed.

While the reasons are largely undocumented, the *Army* album and tour were to be the last Quo projects Colin Johnson worked on. The band decided to fire Johnson – according to Patty Parfitt, but got Alan Crux to deliver the news.

One thing is for certain – Rossi had found a new lease of musical life. He told Derek Oliver in 1986:

> We started off as angry young men – you know, anti-establishment and all that stuff! Fabulous. We may be regarded as establishment now, but that's only because of the mere fact that we're still in business. There's no shame in mellowing you know, and, to be honest, I'm happier with Quo now than I've been for a long time.

Interestingly, around the same time, Parfitt was interviewed by Jon Lewin for *Making Music,* a free publication targeted at amateur and professional musicians alike. Parfitt was quoted as saying:

> ... there was a slight problem with Alan – he had a bit of a gammy right hand, and if you soloed some of his bass parts [on the studio mixing desk]... well, Francis and I had to overdub his bass parts without him knowing to get that real 'chunk'. That's something I haven't told anybody before...

Whether this statement regarding the re-recording of Lancaster's bass lines is true or not, it has since been firmly established that this was not a totally alien way for the band to work. Ironically, we know that Parfitt's vocals had been replaced by Rossi on the Band Aid single and Rossi would later describe in his 2019 memoir that in later years, Francis and Mike Paxman would do their best impressions of Rick singing and playing and use them in lieu of the man himself – sometimes because Rick simply wasn't at the sessions or even replacing his recorded parts due to a sub-par delivery. Rossi even goes as far as to state that Parfitt doesn't even appear at all on a handful of Quo albums but enigmatically doesn't state which.

Rick's statement is upsetting for another reason, too – if Lancaster's 'right hand' issue is accurately described by Parfitt here, it's certainly possible that this was an early symptom of multiple sclerosis, a disease that would afflict Lancaster over the coming decades, and ultimately end his life in September 2021.

1987: The Sun City Debacle

As far as albums and single releases went, 1987 was a quiet year for the band. With the exception of the 'Quo Cake Mix' (a 12" medley of Quo hits cut together by Sanny Xenokottas for a Spanish release) only re-releases of old Quo material surfaced across Europe. Quo delivered a singular *Top of the Pops* appearance for 'Dreamin'' on New Year's Day and spent the rest of the year touring.

After finishing up the current run of shows in the United Arab Emirates in March, Status Quo entered Chipping Norton Studios Towards the back end of April to begin work on what was to become their next album. The band were interviewed about their process for a *Music Box* special on the Super Channel while making the record at Chipping Norton.

Rick Parfitt:

It's true to say you have good days and you have bad days. There's a day where you'll perhaps get two tracks done – in a day – very rare. And when you have a bad day, you can work all day on a backtrack and you won't get it done and it'll take two or three days, as some of the tracks on this album have taken.

By July, the band were touring again, having kicked off the next leg of the tour in Austria. On 29 August, Quo wrapped up the current tour by playing their only UK date that year – the Reading Festival for the fourth time in their career, headlining the second night with support from the likes of Magnum and the Georgia Satellites. During the introduction to this particular version of 'Down Down', Rossi began playing the riff that would become 'Little Dreamer' in 1989 during his opening improvised solo. Interestingly, another riff to come out of similar impromptu sections was 2019's 'Backbone' – Rossi has used these short few minutes of a Quo show to build tension with improvised sections on and off for decades. That Sunday night, Quo delivered a storming set and surprised many hard rock-loving concert-goers who were not expecting much from a band now considered 'cheesy' or unfashionable.

Things had gone swimmingly on the tour until Quo played a run of shows at the Sun City Resort, South Africa, in October 1987 at the behest of manager Alan Crux. Semi-unbeknownst to the band and their crew, the United Nations had called for a cultural boycott of the district – meaning (amongst other sanctions) that musical acts were not to perform there due to race discrimination known colloquially as 'apartheid'. Quo (like others before and after them) had insisted on a desegregated audience and a stage crew of diverse backgrounds, but this was not enough to negate the transgression.

Upon arrival in Johannesburg, the inventor of the idea, Alan Crux, promptly left the band to their own devices while he disappeared off on safari with his wife – much to the chagrin of those left behind until they saw the slice of paradise they'd be working in. Quo lapped up the atmosphere and the exquisite surroundings and lavish casinos, with Francis even enjoying one of his more surprising pastimes – peacefully watching Koi carp.

Quo were not the first to appear in spite of the boycott, and they certainly were not the last. Queen had done the same on their 1984-1985 'The Works' tour and Rod Stewart, Elton John and the Beach Boys had done it a few years earlier. In fact, the list of rule-breakers is surprisingly long, but it was only really Queen and Quo that took the brunt of the flak from the press and the UK Musicians' Union. Even the United Nations themselves saw fit to blacklist both bands for a short while (until they had officially apologised). Quo (and Queen) were made examples of, perhaps fairly, but to suggest the band was racist (as the press were reporting) was preposterous. Not only had Rossi taken his Asian girlfriend Paige with him, but the band had donated to several charitable causes while out there.

Jeff Rich:

> We didn't realise at the time that it was bad. Cliff Richard used to go over every year on the premise that he was doing a 'gospel tour' and he used to get away with it. We had to sign a UN disclaimer to say we wouldn't go back again and we got our wrists slapped. In retrospect, we should never have done it, but nobody said anything at the time. It was a fantastic place though, we had a great time. The people were really friendly.

However, all of the acts had been offered large sums of money from the resort owners to ignore the boycott and over the years, several high-profile acts took the bait. A similar backlash had befallen Paul Simon for his use of South African musicians on his smash hit album *Graceland* the previous year, which was considered a serious violation of the boycott.

The Party Boys

With Lancaster now accepting his fate and no longer w
Quo, he (like Coghlan) had decided to use his show-b
become involved with other projects in his home col
first of which was The Party Boys – a supergroup formed
by Mondo Rock's bassist Paul Christie and guitarist Kevin Borick.
La De Das. The band would adopt a similar flexible line-up as Coghlan's
Diesel band had done but with significantly more commercial success,
perhaps due to the world-class rock royalty that moved through its ranks.
When Lancaster joined in 1986, the line-up consisted of the founders of
the band with Angry Anderson of Rose Tattoo on vocals and guitarist John
Brewster of The Angels, with Christie now on the drum throne. The band
played songs from the individual members' careers alongside known
classic rock favourites from other acts like ZZ Top and The Doors, but for
the duration of Lancaster's tenure never strayed outside of their native
Australia.

Shortly after Lancaster joined, John Swanee (AKA John Swan) replaced
Anderson as the group's frontman and lead vocalist leading to the band's
first and last studio album. The self-titled release came to fruition in
November 1987 and gave the ensemble a number 18 hit on the Australian
album chart. After a respectable opening cover of Argent's 'Hold Your
Head Up', the album's first original track is unleashed – 'Is This The Way
To Say Goodbye'. The track was written primarily by Lancaster (with
contributions from Brewster and Swanee) about the devastating loss
of his friendships in Status Quo and was recorded at Lancaster's newly
purchased Sydney studio 'Earth Media'. It was released as a single in
December 1987 but failed to chart.

Several covers make up the majority of the album's tracklist, with only
three original songs written specifically to split them up. After a cover of
John Kongos' 'He's Gonna Step on You Again' (released as a chart-topping
single by the Party Boys in June 1987), a second Lancaster original is
presented – but one that was never intended to be recorded for the
project. 'She's a Mystery' was written with John Brewster and used for
the 1987 Australian horror movie *Cassandra*. Another original song from
Lancaster, Brewster and Swanee 'Rising Star' makes for one of the catchier
songs on the album and Lancaster's bass is up-front and full of clean,
plectrum-abused character.

The antepenultimate track, 'It Could Have Been You' was a Lancaster
& Skinner composition, originally released as a non-charting single by

...e in 1985. The melody was written exclusively by Skinner as the ...a theme to the Australian movie *An Indecent Obsession* and Lancaster ded the lyrics when the movie producers wanted a hit record to help with the promotion of the film. Lancaster sings the lead vocal on the Party Boys album recording and it is arguably all the better for it.

The album featured several other covers such as Them's 'Gloria', AC/DC's 'High Voltage' and Argent's aforementioned 'Hold Your Head Up', the last of which was another successful single for the Boys, reaching number 21 on the Australian singles chart.

Despite the success of the project, Swanee left to make a movie and Lancaster left to forge his very own group using his newfound musical friends as a springboard into more original music. He would return for a short while in the 1990s but had a creative itch that needed scratching.

1988: Ain't Complaining

Ain't Complaining

Personnel:

Francis Rossi: guitar, vocals

Rick Parfitt: guitar, vocals

John 'Rhino' Edwards: bass guitar

Jeff Rich: drums

Andy Bown: keyboards

Additional Musicians:

Bernie Frost: additional vocals

Paul 'Wix' Wickens: additional keyboards

Graham Preskett: violin

Produced by Pip Williams

Record Label: Vertigo

Recorded: Chipping Norton Studios and Ridge Farm Studios

Release date: 13 June 1988

Highest UK chart place: 12

Running time: 52:16

Side one: 'Ain't Complaining' (Rick Parfitt, Pip Williams) – 4:40, 'Everytime I Think of You' (John Edwards, Jeff Rich, Mike Paxman) – 3:49, 'One for the Money' (Rick Parfitt, Pip Williams) – 4:52, 'Another Shipwreck' (Andy Bown) – 3:48, 'Don't Mind If I Do' (Francis Rossi, John Edwards) – 4:41, 'I Know You're Leaving' (Eric van Tijn, Jochem Fluitsma) – 4:45

Side two: 'Cross That Bridge' (John David) – 3:31, 'Cream of the Crop' (Francis Rossi, Bernie Frost) – 4:03, 'The Loving Game' (Rick Parfitt, John Edwards, Jeff Rich) – 4:23, 'Who Gets the Love?' (Pip Williams, John Goodison) – 5:33, 'Burning Bridges' (Francis Rossi, Andy Bown) – 4:19, 'Magic' (Francis Rossi, Bernie Frost) – 3:52

With *In The Army Now* being the comeback hit Rossi, Parfitt and Phonogram wanted, 1988 was to be the year for the highly anticipated follow-up. Again with Pip Williams in the producer's chair, work began on what would become Quo's eighteenth studio album with a working title of 'The Greatest Fighter' at Chipping Norton. The album was to be named after a Rossi and Frost song of the same name (although sometimes referred to as 'The Fighter') – a song that Rossi would record again for his first solo album 'King of The Doghouse' in 1996. The track was a moody shuffle with a slinky groove but is only slightly marred by more panpipe-sounding synths and a guitar solo that Rossi could have played in his sleep – but as a song, it boasts an interesting lyric and a well-played accompaniment. A couple of other mixes also exist – the best one featuring twin guitars on the introduction. Disappointingly, the record company disliked the song so much that they asked for it to be removed from the release in favour of a ballad – something the album lacked when it was first submitted to Phonogram. With the loss of the song, the whole concept for the album fell through and one of the original ideas for a cover photograph of Mike Tyson was used as a single cover that had nothing to do with the record inside it. Also discussed was a *Sergeant Pepper*-style cover that would depict important political characters from history. A variation of this idea would later be used for the sleeve of the 2000 covers album *Famous in the Last Century*.

In another strange promotional move, Quo temporarily dropped their 20-year Fender Telecaster image and endorsed Charvel/Jackson guitars for all promotional appearances and photoshoots – even though Rossi and Parfitt stuck to their regular Fenders and occasional Gibsons in the studio. Pip Williams and Rhino Edwards may have used the gear in a couple of places, but ultimately, this association was just for show. Again, Quo had their eyes firmly set on cracking America with their new line-up and management and Phonogram felt that 'Album Orientated Rock' was the way to go. Ultimately, it would be the record company that failed the album as far as sales go, but Rossi thinks the quality of the material was the main culprit.

Francis Rossi in the *Ain't Complaining* Deluxe Edition CD liner notes:

> [I was] trying to get everyone to write and make us a band again. I thought everybody should have a share, but of course, you soon realise that allowing each member to contribute 2.5 tracks to the album… well, that's not how a band should be.

The band had to relinquish artistic control of the release several times, and the resulting product was a mixed bag of Quo-brand rock and fad-chasing ersatz pop that scored them a number 12 hit album in the UK – their first studio album to not make the top 10 in 15 years.

The opening title track was written by Parfitt and Williams and features Parfitt's guitar in open G tuning (without a capo). The opening vocal figure pans the audio around the stereo field but in seemingly the wrong places. Williams knew this would confuse listeners but insisted that 'there's nothing right…' came out of the left speaker only and vice-versa because that's exactly what the lyrics described. There's some interesting guitar playing on the track, and the solo is almost certainly Williams on one of the Charvels. Auxiliary vocal features akin to those found on ZZ Top's 'Sharp Dressed Man' also found their way into the track.

Francis Rossi:

> Andrew and I had been fucking about… band humour and shit going on, and we used to talk about some American with a [speech impediment] going 'alwhait' (alright). It went on for fucking weeks and I usually fuck about when I'm doing the vocal and I did it over the intro and Pip [liked it]… and we put it in the sampler, but overall I thought the track, the song, the video was poor.

The song was Quo's first CD single release and reached a disappointing but not disrespectful number 19 on the UK singles charts. A surreal music video starring Griff Rhys Jones with the band is amusing in places but is ultimately another half-hearted attempt at contemporary promotion. It was backed with 'That's Alright' for the CD release – a total re-recording of the Rossi & Frost cut from a few years earlier that benefits from slightly better synth patches and a much cleaner vocal. The shuffle feel delivered by Edwards and Rich is far superior to the original. The 12" single was backed with an extra number, 'Lean Machine' – A Parfitt-penned straight-eight rock song with an undeniable groove but little lyrical soul. It's a piece of craft that showcases Parfitt's ability to layer rhythm guitar parts and deliver a gutsy vocal but is ultimately B-side material that could have made the album with a little finessing of the lyric. There is some athletic harmonica playing courtesy of Bown mixed prominently – a feature that was becoming rare on Quo records at the time.

'Every Time I Think of You' is a commercial-sounding cut from composers Mike Paxman, Rhino Edwards and Jeff Rich. Edwards remains mostly proud of the recording but feels there was something missing and claims that compositionally, the track needed more time spent on it to fix the lack of 'payoff' in the chorus.

John Rhino Edwards:

> I really liked that one – I was surprised that it was never a single. It wasn't quite finished as a song, unfortunately; it was 95 per cent finished. I felt the verses were fantastic and Francis would sing it differently now because I had a vocal that went right across the time,

but at that period, it was all a bit more rigid. Francis is so much looser as a singer now – much more versatile.

While the lyrics and chord sequence may be a touch derivative, the smooth production, the classy delivery of Rossi's vocal and Pip Williams' supersonic guitar solo are far from cliché.

Francis Rossi:

I never ever wanted to be a 'lead' guitarist so if you put a serious guitar player [like Williams] in the room with me, I just think 'oh fucking hell, why don't you just do it!? I haven't got a clue what to do.

Bown's organ on the latter half of the track is one of the better-recorded artefacts of his genius and the overall effect is one of first-rate pop music, but perhaps not in the established Quo vein.

Jeff Rich:

We all worked on all the songs equally as far as I'm concerned – especially arrangement-wise. I wrote a few lines for ['Every Time I Think of You'] which is why we split the credits. A lot of Francis' songs had already been recorded as demos at his home studio and he'd have it all worked out already anyway, and that was pretty much set in stone. We may have added little bits to the arrangement within his framework because some of them were a bit… ropey to start with.

'One for the Money' is a Parfitt and Williams writing collaboration that sees the band in a strange Level 42-like territory with Rhino's bass being doubled by a sequenced bass line and a lightly processed vocal from Parfitt – layered in octaves for extra sonic weight.

John Rhino Edwards:

It's what we thought people wanted. The band was trying to modernise – or at least trying to add another string to the bow!

Despite some interesting imagery, the lyrics serve mainly as a vehicle for the dense arrangement instead of the traditional other way around. A short, twin guitar solo breaks the song up, but the track returns to meandering around the chorus and a strange vocal refrain over the two-chord vamp fade out.

Bown had already recorded and released a single version of 'Another Shipwreck' in 1978 and it featured as the opener on his album *Good Advice* from the same year. Despite being a beautifully crafted song, it never charted and was left well alone until it was suggested for the *Ain't Complaining* sessions ten years later.

Andrew Bown:

[I like 'Another Shipwreck']. Probably technically the best record I've ever made, and the chord progressions still give me goosebumps. Really. On the fade it's as if someone else wrote it... and they're sooo clever... The recording we did with the band was good too. Lot of tension in the track and another great vocal.

It was recorded a whole tone lower to suit Rossi's vocal range – considerably smaller than that of the song's composer. Rossi and Williams' sampler provides another 'alwhait' on the introduction sequence, but the joke is wearing thin by this point in proceedings. Compositionally, it's a song that would have been better suited to Barry Manilow, Kenny Rogers, Leo Sayer or even a late-career Genesis. It is harmonically adventurous, frequently modulating with expressive suspensions, quirky inversions, complex internal and assonance rhymes in the lyrics and has a driving '80s disco feel to boot. While Quo make an excellent job of it, the song does not play to their strengths and the sophisticated elements simply don't suit the band's then brand of pop rock.

Francis Rossi in the *Ain't Complaining* Deluxe Edition CD liner notes in 2018:

It's a magical song, but for us... again maybe we were drifting away from the original Quo-type stuff. That's the problem with his material, I find – you record it and love its quirky Andrew-ness, but for some inexplicable reason, the public doesn't always like it.

'Don't Mind If I Do' is among Rhino's first writing credits with a member of Status Quo. It was written with Rossi at the guitarist's house in Surrey and was developed over a small number of writing sessions.

John Rhino Edwards:

That was back in the day when people wrote together in the same room. We never did a demo of that song – we just routined that in the studio, but I think we had that pretty sussed. Myself, Francis and Andrew tend to write remotely nowadays…

Edwards later composed a synthesised cello part that's only barely audible after the band crash into the introduction, and it is one of Rossi's favourite elements of the record. The heavily syncopated vocal (doubled with acoustic guitars) commands attention and makes for an effective hook.

'I Know You're Leaving' is the first ballad of the album and is one of the weaker tracks by far, and was recorded at Ridge Farm Studios at the behest of Phonogram after the initial album sessions had taken place at Chipping Norton.

Written by Dutch composers Eric van Tijn and Jochem Fluitsma, the song was forced upon the band because the record company believed a ballad was needed for a single. Next to the other songs on the album, it seems insipid and drab, but given to a band like Chicago or REO Speedwagon, it could have been a hit. It's easy to hear that the band's heart isn't in it and the recording makes for the most vapid cut on the album. Rossi delivers a solid but unemotional vocal and instead of ripping into a heart-wrenching guitar solo, we are treated to a perfunctory four-bar break of un-imaginative instrumental filler. The fretless bass part allegedly proved too tricky for Edwards, who eventually ended up performing it on a Moog synthesiser.

'Cross That Bridge' is a catchy composition from John David that Edwards believes would have been a hit single – the band even mimed to the track on a couple of Spanish TV appearances, which could imply the record company also believed in its potential. Keen listeners will spot a subtle bass overdub from Rhino on the opening notes of the main riff – his Status Series 2000 into a fuzzbox and into a Marshall stack is doubling the descending guitar line. Rossi spent a day recording the vocal while fighting off a flu virus and so the finished vocal is compiled of several takes stitched together by Williams. Celebrated UK session musician Graham Preskett plays live fiddle on this track and it adds considerable authenticity to the country-flavoured song where a synth would have achieved the opposite. A quirky guitar break provided by Rossi temporarily breaks into a two-part harmony before the innocent melodic refrain returns to play the track out.

'Cream of the Crop' is a Rossi/Frost composition that was another contender for a single but was later dropped from such discussions once the record company deemed it 'too fast'. The song opens with a sentimental quasi-rubato keyboard solo before the band crash into the song at a pacey 174 beats per minute; putting it among Quo's fastest recordings of the decade. While the vocal melody is catchy, the lyrics are quaint and do the song very few favours, with the title being the biggest offender in this regard. Rossi delivers one of his finest falsetto vocals with perhaps his highest note on record during the 'Rosalie' bridge – a high A climbing up to a B-flat. Even more impressive is Bernie Frost's harmony (mixed quite low) that sees him hit the C and D above Rossi's lead vocal. Rhino and Rich steal the show here with some of their tightest playing on any Quo record. Edwards plays metronomic 8th notes with his fingers rather than a plectrum and Rich matches him step for step – a masterful rhythm section indeed.

Jeff Rich:

Francis was more particular about his tracks. He'd want a certain rhythm and that was it – he didn't want us to experiment because he knew exactly what he wanted, but I never felt restricted by Quo. It was playing live that I loved most anyway – you could really let yourself go.

After a respectable twin lead guitar solo, a vulgar synthesised horn section plays an eight-bar solo break before another mono synth (akin to the one found on 'Marguerita Time') plays a legato line that is nicely conceptualised but feels like way too much after what preceded it. It was played live on the album tour but was dropped the following year.

'The Loving Game' is a track that Rhino would have happily left on the demo cassette as he believes it to be the worst set of lyrics he'd ever written. Co-written with Parfitt and Rich, the lyrics are definitely not up to the standard that the bassist would later hold himself to, but as an instrumental, the track leaves little to be desired – it's one of only a handful of tracks recorded during these sessions that actually 'rocks' and Parfitt's vocal breaks up at the top of his chest range – where many think he sings the best.

John Rhino Edwards:

An awful song. The worst song I ever wrote with Status Quo, I think. What a pile of shit. It's so lyrically dull – I hate lines like 'straight down the line… I really need you tonight… your body next to mine!?' Fuck off! If you like that song, you're ill.

Jeff Rich:

> 'The Loving Game'… not the best track in the world. Rick came up with
> the riff, I think, and we all helped finish it. Not the ideal track, really.
> I think it was more a case of just putting one of Rick's songs on the
> album…

When the band were asked to return to the studio to record some slower
cuts for a potential single, producer Williams threw his composition 'Who
Gets the Love?' into the mix. Written with John Goodison (notable for
his own work as a singer, producer and writer), the track was released as
a single and just made the top 40 at number 34 on the UK singles chart
in 1988, backed by Parfitt's 'Halloween'. The composition is significantly
better crafted than 'I Know You're Leaving' and is slightly more suited to
the band. Rossi seems more at home with the vocals and Parfitt is given
the middle eight section as a lead vocalist. While the guitar solo found
on the album and single version is a solid but by-numbers placeholder,
the solo from Williams on the 12" mix is among his finest ever recorded.
Possibly his Stratocaster, the tone is clean and glassy and the motivic
development is pure artistry – he leaves vast amounts of space for each
phrase to breathe and the closing bars contrast this approach with a
beautifully executed melodic sequence that builds excitement and follows
the harmony.

John Rhino Edwards:

> [That session] was very long-winded. Pip had written that song with John
> Goodison – a really weird writing combination. [Goodison] was a Tin
> Pan Alley-style writer. It was a real lot of work, that one. It was the full Pip
> production – very clean, good sounds and bang in tune.

A music video directed by prolific music video maker Mike Brady featured
the band in their most cinematic and serious promo footage. The video
has a moody charm and definite American aesthetic that was intended to
reach an adult contemporary audience across the pond, albeit to no avail.
Like 'Cream of the Crop', the song was played on the tour but never again
performed live by the band. The 12" mix was backed with the additional
track 'The Reason for Goodbye' – another Williams/Goodison composition
with later credits granted to Parfitt and Rossi for their extra lyrical and
melodic input in the studio. It's another track of exceptional production

quality and seems to hark back to elements of Quo's earlier style – boogie guitars, bluesy piano interjections, a catchy melodic chorus – and a slide guitar solo from Williams is a welcome addition to the track. With the exception of the drum machine cymbals, this track could have easily been a single that screamed 'Quo' to the record-buying public. The CD single also featured a real Quo curiosity – 'The Wanderer (The Sharon the Nag Mix)'. It's the exact same recording as the one released in 1984 but with Kircher's drums and Lancaster's bass replaced with Rich and Edwards, respectively. It's likely that Phonogram wanted some old hits used as B-sides to help single sales and the original multitracks were still in the possession of Williams and Rossi for 'The Wanderer'. With Rossi wanting more and more distance put between the old line up and the new, it's a possibility that he re-recorded the bass and drums to remove Lancaster from the song. The version that still receives airplay is almost always the original '84 master, but Rossi doesn't even remember this second version at all.

Francis Rossi:

> Sharon the WHAT!? No idea. That title sounds like an anagram to me, but I think I'd have remembered re-recording those parts?

John 'Rhino' Edwards:

> It does sound a lot like me, in fact, I'd say that is me. When I think back, I have the vaguest of memories it was something Jeff and I knocked out late at night at Chipping Norton when we were recording *Ain't Complaining*.

'Burning Bridges (On And Off And On Again)' was written by Andy Bown and Francis Rossi at a hotel room in Gothenburg and perplexed the rest of the band when they heard the demo – Edwards didn't even think it was B-side material and the record executive at Phonogram initially agreed.

John Rhino Edwards:

> I remember recording 'Burning Bridges' really well because I thought 'what is this shit!?'... how wrong was I!? I love it now and I think the drumming is very good on that track.

The instrumental jig is based on an old English folk jig/quadrille called Darby Kelly. Bown first heard the tune after hearing his daughter playing the tune on her recorder after a lesson. Once he found out that the tune was old enough to be out of copyright, he used it for the song he had written with Rossi, although the opening melodic motif is the work of the Quo writers themselves. Apparently, Bown recorded all of his keyboard parts in one take – a moment captured by Parfitt on his camcorder that has sadly never been seen by the public. Once Quo and Williams recorded the track, the rest of the band started to see the song's potential and the reaction at gigs was so strong that the record company reconsidered its release and it became a number five hit for the group for Christmas 1988.

Jeff Rich, talking on *Metalville.co.uk* in 2015:

> There's certain tracks that you record and after you've recorded, think, 'That sounds like a record'. Some don't. Like 'Burning Bridges' – it's great. As soon as we recorded that and we were listening to it back, we thought, 'That sounds good. That's going to be a hit'. You can tell. There are certain tracks that you know would be successful. There's some that maybe you think won't become successful.

The song has a strong triplet feel that plays into the group's penchant and talent for medium-paced shuffles and again features violinist Graham Preskett doubling the synth parts on his fiddle. British rock band Muse have since been known to incorporate the jig into their live shows and Irish folk group Foster and Allen released the song with rising country singer Nathan Carter as a single in 2017. A seemingly low-budget music video was filmed to promote the single and it featured the band surrounded by a circular Dolly track to capture them in a light-hearted scene of mimed performance and their hired Scottish dancers.

Francis Rossi in *Down Down the Decades*:

> I enjoyed [filming] that. All the cameramen were going around in kilts and stuff – I don't know whose idea that was. I had to keep stopping because I'd only be able to turn around once or twice before I was gonna start throwing up. I'd have to go back the other way or stop for a while…

The album version features an extra verse at the beginning of the song that was cut to keep the single time down. The 12" cover featured a shot of boxer Mike Tyson – a strange choice but one that was perhaps financially necessary. The photo was meant to be for the album cover (when it was titled *The Fighter*), but once the usage had been paid for, the title and tracklisting of the album changed. 'Burning Bridges' has been a regular feature of the live set since they incorporated it into the repertoire during the back end of the 1988 tour and it was included on the first *Aquostic* album in 2014.

Even more surprisingly, Bown and Edwards rewrote the lyrics to transform the song into 'Come on You Reds', a 1994 number one hit for the band's collaboration with Manchester United FC. Rossi asked Edwards to help Bown with the lyrics as he was much more knowledgeable about football. In an attempt to follow up on the success, the band collaborated with the team a second time on 'We're Gonna Do It Again' – a hip-hop reworking of Quo's 1978 hit 'Again and Again' that was not quite as popular, making it to number 15 in 1995.

The album closes with 'Magic', a Rossi and Frost tune that finishes the record with another middle-of-the-road, ear-friendly pop song. The opening and recurring brass synths date the record and the vocal processing and gated reverb of Rich's snare drum act as willing accomplices. While the production choices of the day may be no longer welcome in the 21st century, the melodic hooks certainly are and they come in the form of the vocal melody and Williams' nylon string classical guitar solo.

Francis Rossi:

I thought it was a bit of a shame, that album… Rick got people to write with him because he got lazy, I suppose. Rick wrote great little ballads and again, part of the affectation of him being 'rawk', was that he didn't want to write those songs [anymore]. If you check out the stuff from early on, Rick wrote ballads which were great – it was Rick! The other stuff was Rick trying to be something else which was frustrating to me.

Rick Parfitt in *Classic Rock* Magazine in March 2017:

The music was too polite… There was no weight behind what we were doing. The edge had gone; we weren't real anymore.

Jeff Rich:

There was a lot of politics involved in Quo's studio sessions – everyone wanted their own tracks on the albums. Consequently, some tracks ended up on albums that probably shouldn't have.

In August 2020, Rhino revealed in an interview with Paul Bruns that during the early sessions for the album, Pip Williams suggested a song called 'You're the Voice' – a record by Australian singer John Farnham that he had heard, liked and saw the potential in it for a Quo single. The song hadn't hit in the UK and Pip saw an opening. Rossi, however, maintains that it was he and Rhino who first saw the potential in the song in the catering tent on the 'Army' tour.

Francis Rossi:

> Colin Johnson… he'd just got his son a gig at Warner Brothers or whoever it was who had that [song's publishing]. They'd released that thing twice and it had died, so when we checked it out, I said, 'bitchin' – it's been out, it's died, we'll have that – we'll change the key', I could never sing as well as Farnham… We were ready to make it for the next album and the fucking thing took off…

Unfortunately, just as Quo began work on the track, the Farnham version became a smash hit worldwide and so Quo abandoned the idea. Interestingly, Williams would produce the track again with Tobias Boshell for Scottish singer Brenda Cochrane for her album *The Voice* – her sobriquet. Rossi, Frost and Rhino all make appearances on the album and it's highly likely that her version was born out of Quo's sequenced demo, although this rumour has never been confirmed either way.

Following the success of Live Aid in 1986, Bob Geldof and his money-raising team changed tactics and decided on a sports-themed fundraising campaign. 'Sport Aid' raised $37 million and was a huge success and so when the opportunity for another event came up in 1988, Quo were asked to re-record 'Rocking All Over the World' with a slightly altered title and lyrics. 'Running All Over the World' was recorded in only one day at Chipping Norton under the supervision of Pip Williams, who produced Quo's first recording in 1977.

John Rhino Edwards:

> We were in the middle of a tour and we went to Chipping Norton and recorded that in about an hour. We may have even been on our way to a gig, actually.

The song was a fairly successful hit, making number 17 on the UK Singles Chart, but, more useful to the band, it gave them the opportunity to record the standard lyrics also – meaning that any mimed playback performances would include Rhino and Rich. The re-recording is far superior to the 1977 version, with better performances in the rhythm section, a punchier mix and a whimsical video that featured all five members of the band and no string puppets replacing the bassist – unlike the original 1977 video.

The accompanying 'Complaining' tour kicked off in Cork, Ireland, in May 1988 – around a month before the album hit the shelves. The setlist was notable for opening with 'Whatever You Want' – the song normally reserved for the string of big hits at the end of a gig had exchanged places with 'Caroline'.

Quo had taken flak for playing in Sun City the previous year but received none at all for playing a run of shows in communist Moscow at their Olympic hall as part of their Sport Aid obligations, where they were greeted with flowers by local school children. Once the band realised that a language barrier prevented the audience from letting themselves go, Rossi requested that an Olympic signboard ask for the polite but reserved audience's participation. Once they had been given permission to enjoy themselves, the 17,000-strong audience became just like any Quo audience on earth – loud, content and appreciative. After the unprecedented run of 14 sold-out dates in Russia in August, Bown came down with pneumonia and so the band cancelled several European shows and took the month of September off, returning in November to continue in Austria, and finishing the run in London in time for Christmas. Support for the majority of the tour in the UK and Germany was provided by Canadian rockers Honeymoon Suite.

Also, in 1988, German singer Stephan Remmler hired Edwards and Rich to record on his song 'Drei Weiße Birken' ('Three White Birches'), but Edwards believed he only hired them so that Rossi would become involved. What emerged is one of Quo's strangest records and the first of several obscure collaborations to follow in the coming decades. Produced by Remmler, the song's lilting shuffle certainly lends itself to Quo's brand of laid-back boogie and Rossi is afforded a 16-bar solo that, by the sound of it, may have genuinely been one of the seldom played Charvel guitars appearing in the promo video.

Francis Rossi

What a shit solo! I was embarrassed about that. He came over to the UK and I just dropped the solo and some backing vocals on. Terrible.

The promo film is a surreal viewing experience but does show Remmler and Quo (including Parfitt who did not play on the record) – with the band often as bemused as the fan base was at the strangeness of the project – enjoying their time together. While the single didn't fare so well, the album it was included on (*lotto*) peaked at number 36 on the Official German Albums Chart. The song itself would almost certainly have had a stronger commercial life as a Eurovision entry.

The Bombers

In 1988, Lancaster formed the aptly named Bombers – a hard rock band with blues undertones and glossy pop rock production. The band featured ex-bandmate Coghlan on drums as well as Party Boy John Brewster on rhythm guitar, Steve Crofts of Topaz on lead guitar, and singer Tyrone Coates on lead vocal and sax.

This line up was fairly unheard in recorded format until a live show from May 1989 was released in 2019 by Barrel and Squidger Records. The band are powerfully tight here with a heavy energy that clearly suited the touring acts of the day as the Bombers were repeatedly asked to open for the likes of Cheap Trick, Alice Cooper and Skid Row, but the band's main raison d'etre was in the pub rock circuit under their own name to build a dedicated domestic following.

Managed by Bob Young, this (mostly) Australian band would go on to be signed to US label A&M Records and release a studio album *Aim High* (featuring a much better recording of 'Is This The Way to Say Goodbye') in 1990, but by this point, Coghlan had left the band, with Lancaster citing that his style of playing wasn't quite the right fit for the group. The album didn't fare too well either, with A&M being acquired by Phonogram before any real promotional undertakings were completed.

The Bombers went on to perform under various names and with various line-ups until 1997, but while they had quite the underground following for live shows and ample respect from their contemporaries, they never really made headway as a successful recording band.

1989: Perfect Remedy

Perfect Remedy

Personnel:

Francis Rossi: guitar, vocals

Rick Parfitt: guitar, vocals

John 'Rhino' Edwards: bass guitar

Jeff Rich: drums

Andy Bown: keyboards

Produced by Pip Williams

Record Label: Vertigo

Recorded: Compass Point Studios, Nassau, Summer 1989

Release date: 17 November 1989

Highest UK chart place: 49

Running time: 47:00

Side one: 'Little Dreamer' (Francis Rossi, Bernie Frost) – 4:04, 'Not at All' (Francis Rossi, Bernie Frost) – 2:54, Heart On Hold' (Andy Bown, Phil Palmer) – 3:36, 'Perfect Remedy' (Francis Rossi, Bernie Frost) – 4:36, Address Book' (Francis Rossi, Bernie Frost) – 3:37, 'The Power of Rock' (Rick Parfitt, Pip Williams, Francis Rossi) – 6:04

Side two: 'The Way I Am' (John Edwards, Jeff Rich, Mike Paxman) – 3:35, 'Tommy's in Love' (Francis Rossi, Bernie Frost) – 3:01, 'Man Overboard' (Rick Parfitt, Pip Williams) – 4:29, 'Going Down for the First Time' (Andy Bown, John Edwards) – 4:00, Throw Her a Line' (Francis Rossi, Bernie Frost) – 3:34, '1000 Years' (Francis Rossi, Bernie Frost) – 3:31

With Williams now firmly established as the producer, Quo needed to make hits in the 1980s, the band departed (as suggested by Parfitt) for Compass Point Studios in Nassau in the summer of 1989 to make the album that would become *Perfect Remedy* – a fitting title to hopefully put them back on a streak of top 10 albums.

Colin Johnson, trusted manager and confidant to Rossi, was now no longer working with Status Quo at all. After allegedly re-mortgaging his house several times over the years to pay the crew and band, he had served his 17 years. Alan Crux had also departed the company, leaving just Iain Jones to look after the band himself. Desperate to sort out the band's finances once and for all, he contacted David Walker of the Handle Group – a management company that looked after the affairs of producer Pip Williams among others. Despite his initial shock at how finances had been dealt with up to this point, Walker soon took the band on, and immediately began to straighten things out, but not all members of the band were pleased with his presence.

Jeff Rich:

> When David Walker came in, [morale] went from bad to worse. He only ever had time for Francis and Rick. He wasn't interested in the rest of the band at all. When we all used to share a dressing room, we'd be sitting all together, he'd walk straight past me, Rhino and Andrew as if we weren't there. He'd pat Francis and Rick on the back… his nose was so far up their arse it was unbelievable. He was doing it for his own benefit. He took the band on so that he could make a lot of money. He turned the band against [their previous management].

By this point, the band's use of cocaine and alcohol was severely impeding their ability to write and record within a tight timeframe and the luxuries afforded to them by the Bahamas-based studio served as a welcome distraction to the fact that the material they were taking out there was not strong enough to make a hit album with. Additionally, every member of the band brought their families with them (except Rossi and Bown) and so leaving wives, girlfriends and kids playing in the sunny pool to go make an album did not seem so attractive. Parfitt and his now-pregnant wife Patty even went out ahead of the band for a short belated honeymoon.

The studio had been founded in 1977 by Chris Blackwell – owner of Island Records, and when built, was home to several artists while they made hit albums – such as Dire Straits' *Communiqué*, AC/DC's *Back in Black* and no fewer than three Iron Maiden albums (*Piece of Mind*, *Powerslave* and *Somewhere in Time*) – and the artists would often stay in the surrounding cottages while working in paradise. Unfortunately, by the time Quo arrived in 1989, the studio was up for sale after the head engineer Alex Sadkin was killed in a tragic car accident a few years before, aged just 38. With nobody to look after the day-to-day running of the facilities, the studio fell into disrepair. While a renovation in the early 1990s proved fruitful and breathed new life into the workspace, the studio closed for good in 2010 – with a lot of the equipment and spaces left to rot.

While out in the Bahamas, the band ran into David Bowie's Tin Machine, who were recording their eponymous debut album at the same studio, and they socialised for a short time – but it was soon clear that Tin

Machine had a much stronger work ethic than Quo at the time. Cocaine and alcohol were even more readily available than they were in England and Parfitt especially took full advantage of the platter of narcotics on offer. In fact, Quo's initial sessions were so unproductive that the album had to be finished at Comfort's Place Studios in Surrey upon returning to the UK after almost three months in the Caribbean.

The album cover was conceived by Bown and hand-drawn by artist Karl Lloyd but all to little avail – the album peaked at number 49 on the UK Albums Chart, making it Quo's first major studio album flop since their experimental marijuana-induced boogie-blues transition album *Dog of Two Head* in 1971. It fared slightly better in Sweden, Switzerland and Australia, but the record is still considered to be the lowest point of their '80s career.

The album opens with 'Little Dreamer' – a Rossi and Frost composition that opens with a similar chordal riff as 'Down Down' although played in a higher octave, different key, and also played in standard tuning.

Francis Rossi:

> I'd been to Bernie Frost's house and it [the opening riff] came out straight away and we thought it was great. We said 'fucking marvellous, we just need a melody' and Bernie's son was singing [to what would become the opening vocal melody] 'I need a day off, I need a bleedin' day off'. I was disappointed with that single at the time – when we were writing it, we weren't trying hard enough on the verses. It kinda slows down in the meterage but now when I hear the chorus, I think it's fucking excellent.

The song trundles along in typical straight-eight fashion, with Parfitt and Rossi singing the first verse in their trademark two-part harmony. There's several hooks present in the song, many of them taking place over borrowed chords and modulations. The lyrics are not particularly thought-provoking or artistic, but do seem to serve the contours of the melody and give the song a certain commercial charge allowing listeners to pick up the basic vowel sounds after just one listen. Some of the overdubbed synthesisers have proved with time to be an unwise choice, especially as the bass synths are playing lines and fills that could have been beautifully executed by Edwards instead. A synthesised horn section enters during the second half of the song and somewhat cheapens the overall effect where a real section would have added a welcome third dimension to the recording. There's some fine lead guitar work from Rossi here also that does not fall into the traps that some of his previous efforts have. He takes a simple melodic idea and develops it with variation and ornamentation with one of his best-driven guitar sounds on record. There's some nicely recorded acoustic guitar overdubs that gallop through active instrumental sections with a rhythmic accuracy that only Parfitt could achieve. The changes of pace, while interesting and musical, would not have served this song's viability as a single well. The sections can feel disconnected and if you aren't paying attention, could sound like different songs. While some of the aesthetic choices of the day (such as the heavy delay effect on the vocal) have not aged so well, you can't fault the playing and imagination that went into the arrangement. The music video for the single featured the band playing outside of a young woman's house while she slept, which is even more 'on the nose' than the original lyrics and adds a certain uneasiness to the release as a whole. The single was released in December 1989 and peaked at number 79 on the UK singles charts, making it the biggest flop of Quo's professional commercial career. It was performed during the first half of Quo's setlist on the Perfect Remedy tour but was dropped the following year. The 7" single was backed with 'Rotten to the Bone', a Rossi and Bown tune that is both humorous and ferocious in equal measure. The song modulates rapidly between sections and motors ahead in a style that could only be Status Quo's. The song opens in half time and features some excellent drumming from Jeff Rich and his flurries of semiquaver bass drum fills. In fact, Rich's drumming is very much the star of the show throughout the track, especially during the chorus sections, played in double time with his snare drum work executed to a level that few British drummers are capable of. Co-composer Bown leans heavily on his established repertoire of honky-tonk licks and Jerry Lee Lewis-style glissandi giving the song a country flavour that Rossi would definitely have approved of. A three-part tag ends the song before an abrupt concerted ending phrase leaving the listener feeling like they could have done with another refrain. The 12" and CD single releases featured the Parfitt and Williams cut 'Doing It All For You', a fast swinging country boogie track that could have been better received with dirtier sounding guitars instead of clean electrics and DI'd acoustics. It's highly possible that this track was recorded on top of the demo recorded by Williams and Parfitt in the UK before leaving for Compass Point – replacing the demo elements piecemeal with the full band.

'Not at All' is a bluesy shuffle from the pen of Francis Rossi and Bernie Frost that was released as the first single from the album in October 1989 but only reached number 50 on the UK Singles Chart, making it Quo's first commercial failure in several years. While the track is notable for some impressive bass and organ playing and several favourable reviews at the time, the song did little to impress either the fanbase or the public – a result possibly aided by the bizarre music video that seems improvised on the day of filming and again in the edit suite in lieu of storyboarding any relevant ideas.

Francis Rossi:

> I insisted on that as a single, but when it came to doing it live, it was too fucking high to sing – fine in the studio but too high to sing live. Our manager didn't think it would be a hit, and up until then, I'd basically chosen all the singles. He warned me that if I got this one wrong... they'd had a remake of *Juke Box Jury* and Siouxsie Sioux (her band were great, but she was just full of herself) said it was dangerous, this record – really badly panned it. Although the record barely moved, I thought it was magic... but it didn't work.

The song was not unanimously denounced by the panel on the 1989 show chaired by Jools Holland, but only boxer Frank Bruno truly stuck up for the band and Spandau Ballet frontman Tony Hadley heavily lambasted the production, but the 'jury' was hung by the end of the discussion. It was released with the Bown composition 'Gone Thru the Slips' on the B-side – a two-feel country rock song that details a high-maintenance love interest around heavy-handed synthesiser sounds that should have been played on guitar or fiddle. Bown's harmonies are audible throughout under Rossi's lead vocal. It's a charming cut but let down by the constrictive technological production equipment of the day.

'Heart On Hold' is a song written by Andy Bown and celebrated UK session guitarist Phil Palmer, who also worked as a guitarist with Bown on his 1983 release 'Help Me' along with drummer Stewart Copeland of the Police. The song relies heavily on technological metaphor and cliché yet still remains one of the more interesting songs on the album, possibly due to the fact that it is so different to everything else on it, both rhythmically and melodically. There's more space on this song than perhaps any other Status Quo song in their whole career, with Rhino and Rich playing in a quasi-reggae one-drop feel.

Andrew Bown:

'Heart On Hold' was a total co-write with Phil Palmer. My music room, a few drugs and straight down to work – cool demo. We'd like to have recorded it properly and released it as a single, but no one we knew was interested, so I sold it to the band and we did a pretty good job on it, although it would probably have suited many other bands better – it wasn't very 'Quo' was it?

Parfitt's harmonies are mixed quite high and so his counter-melodies are brought out at just the right moment. In hindsight, the song would have perhaps benefitted from fewer sound effects such as those found at the line 'We can make a spark with the right connection…' Rossi delivers a minimalist but powerful-sounding solo over a rather sparse backing arrangement, with the clear sound of his Steinberger guitar and Marshall amplifier in the live room at Compass Point on full show. Pip Williams also left his fingerprints on some of the guitar overdubs, such as the ascending electric guitar line in the final verse.

The title track is a medium-paced shuffle that may be melodically too pretty to please fans of their '70s output, but it is definitely performed at a level any professional musician could be proud of. The feel here really swings and Parfitt's rhythm guitars seem to float effortlessly atop the solid foundation of both Edwards and Rich. Another song from the prolific writing team of both Rossi and Frost, the song explores Rossi's love of Irish and Scottish Ionian mode melodies played across a triplet-based rhythm, a la Burning Bridges and live versions of Roadhouse Blues. The melodic cadences are incredibly satisfying to the ear and when Rossi breaks away from them for his exceptional guitar solo, their return is welcomed with open arms. The song closes with two repeating chords the way that a classical symphony would conclude – a repeating cadence that composers like Beethoven and Mozart would have used early in their careers. Although not released a single, it did find its way into the live set, where it remained for the duration of the *Perfect Remedy* tour.

'Address Book' is the fifth track on the album and is a country-flavoured shuffle written by Rossi and Frost. Composed in the same vein as 'Invitation' and 'Dirty Water', it did not receive favourable reviews from hardened fans due to its soft production values and overly romantic lyrical content.

John Rhino Edwards:

I never really liked that track 'Address Book', but Francis adored it. I didn't understand the appeal of that one. He doesn't write these songs to please anybody, he just loves country music.

The second verse features some pretty double-stopped quasi-Italian sounding lines from Pip Williams that do nothing to harden the sound, but add a soupçon of sophistication to an otherwise conservative recording. It is rumoured that it is still a favourite of Rossi's, despite the rest of the band claiming indifference towards it and the majority of the classic fanbase detesting it.

Curiously, it was performed by Rossi and Parfitt in an acoustic setting backed by a string orchestra on Richard Digance's TV show *Abracadigance* in 1990, with the host accompanying the pair with his own brand of Travis-picked guitar accompaniment and even trading lead vocal duties with Rossi.

Closing the first side is the album's longest cut and most respected of all recordings present on the release.

John Rhino Edwards:

Pip had a lot of control – even more so on *Perfect Remedy*. I think it's a pretty lifeless album with weak material. The nearest thing to a good one on there is probably 'The Power of Rock'. As for my musical opinion and advice … at the time, it wasn't as sought as it later became. I might have looked like a twat, but I was playing great!

Composed by Rossi, Parfitt and Williams, 'The Power of Rock' is an epic celebration of Quo's ability to write a catchy stadium anthem with dynamic changes of pace, multiple melodic hooks and instrumental passages just exciting enough to please even the hardcore fans. The song does seem like an attempt to rewrite the band's 1973 album track 'Forty-five Hundred Times', albeit with a fresher production and stronger melody but with Rick using the same BBDGBE tuning. Rossi's lyrics were originally inspired by the troubles in Northern Ireland – hence the original title, 'Fighting for Love'. The anthemic 'woah's were included at the behest of Williams so as to once again emulate 'You're the Voice' by John Farnham.

Pip Williams, posted on the *SQMB* on 11 January 2009:

I'm proud to say that most of the song structure was mine. Rick contributed strongly to his middle vocal section ('But they were learning' etc). I had the other melodies, riffs and most of the lyrics in place and the guys helped me to tidy them up. Frame is great at finding lovely melodic twists and turnarounds. I remember that I wanted to book rehearsal time to really work the song in, but that wasn't possible before we left for Nassau. I'd put together a pretty good demo in any case. It was recorded as a single backing track and I sang the guide vocal in the studio. The guys played all their own parts and Frame's extended solos were spontaneous (he'd not yet lost the enthusiasm for playing long solos!). This is some of the best improvised soloing Frame ever did on any of the songs I recorded with them, and the piano solo is a belter too. We got a few people in to sing the chorus – crew and others. I think they turned in brilliant live performances of it later. It's always easy to say that they play certain songs better live (such as ['Burning Bridges']), but the simple truth is – of course, they do, they were still learning them when they were recorded!

Edwards plays a simple repeating pedal-tone bass line locked perfectly with Rich's bass drum but occasionally adding melodic flourishes that are as propulsive as they are artistic. Lead vocals are shared between Rossi and Parfitt, and while Rossi's guitar solos get an honourable mention, it is Bown's piano solo towards the back end of the track that is the highlight of the piece. 'The Power of Rock' was added to the live setlist for the '89 tour, but was dropped the year after due to loss of relevancy and a tepid reception from floating fans. Originally intended as a single release, the idea was abandoned – due to the record company's (and David Walker's) increasing concern around promoting releases that would not see a large enough financial return.

The Edwards, Rich, and Mike Paxman composition 'The Way I Am' is an inoffensive middle-of-the-road rock shuffle that is occasionally maudlin but consistently grooving. It opens with some behind-the-beat twin guitar lead playing from Pip Williams and features a tasteful but restrained guitar solo from Rossi.

John Rhino Edwards:

I love the groove on that, but it's lyrically a bit inept – even by my own low standards.

The slow 12/8 ballad 'Tommy's in Love' was written by Rossi and Frost and is considered by some as the worst Status Quo song written to date. The song served as proof that this was now definitely Francis Rossi's band and he was beginning to form attachments to songs he knew would disinterest the band and infuriate the fanbase. Adding proverbial insult to injury, Rossi would insist on a re-recording of this track for the follow-up album 'Rock till You Drop' but, while improved by production, the song was equally as disliked by Quo's record-buying fans and the song was never so much as mentioned again except for a feature in *Record Collector* with John Reed:

> I thought I'd got it wrong the first time but still didn't get it right. It's one of those mistakes you make. I sometimes fall in love with my songs.

The song's lyrical content is considerably more saccharin than any of Rossi's others, detailing an Americanised cliché love story between two young sweethearts. Synthesised pizzicato strings, unfortunately, do little to redeem the Buddy Holly-esque song, although several brownie points are earned in the 1991 re-recordings guitar solo.

Whilst some of the aesthetic choices haven't aged well, it's hard not to like the performances from all five members of the band and the lyrics that are relatable and whimsical on the track 'Man Overboard' (written by Parfitt and Williams). Rhino, again, provides a pedal point accompaniment over shifting harmonies provided by the rest of the band. Williams delivers lead guitar passages over the fade-out that appear to be harmonised digitally rather than being multi-tracked, resulting in a glitchy, clashy effect that's unusual for the band.

Jeff Rich:

> When I first joined the band, it was reasonably loose – we'd use the take with the best feel. But as time went on, everything was being recorded to a click which meant that nobody could speed up or slow down. It worked OK, but the main problem with a click is that it takes all the excitement out of it because, in rock music, you want the music to breathe. You may speed up a little for a guitar solo and bring it back down again for the verse – barely noticeable but impossible with a click track.

'Going Down for the First Time' ranks among one of Rhino's more poetic lyrics from this period and it was written with keyboardist Andy Bown.

Under the influence of Rossi and producer Williams, the track was gently countrified.

John Rhino Edwards:

> I originally wanted it to be a bit more Beatle-y than it turned out because it came out quite country and western – Francis loves country music.

The song features an effective backing vocal arrangement by Williams, complete with harmonies and sliding glissando lines that frame the lyrics in an artistic and prosodic way. Rossi's favourite synthesised fiddle sound is back, but tastefully a little lower in the mix and doubled by an electric guitar. The guitar solo is simple but appropriate, played on the lower strings with a hint of chorus and tremolo. Although some listeners have since claimed that this song contains pedal steel guitar, it does not. It simply features overdubs played by Pip Williams on standard electric guitar in a quasi-steel guitar style.

The penultimate cut, 'Throw Her a Line', is a Rossi and Frost composition that features obscure synth patch choices combined with a pretty melody and chord sequence, although the lyrics lack sophistication in favour of sing-ability. The overdriven guitar solo halfway through the track is expertly delivered by Rossi, with his legato playing well and truly in the spotlight. The song would have made a much stronger cut given a more creative introduction, and a smaller reliance on synthesisers and over-dramatised vocal processing. By this point in Quo's career, Rossi was very much abandoning Quo's penchant for blues-inflected melodies, now preferring instead to rely on the diatonic scale tones of the home key.

Francis Rossi:

> We would never steer away from anything that was coming out of our gobs. Writing with Bob [Young]… when he's improvising the vocal melody, he would stick to the pentatonic [5 note] scale or a blues scale, but me and Bernie [liked the sound of the whole major scale] – almost nursery rhyme-like if you will.

The closing ballad '1000 Years' is a genuinely beautifully crafted piece of musical art. It features Quo's most elaborate chord sequence ever on record and is lyrically among Rossi's strongest. While definitely not a fan favourite, the song could have easily been a hit for an artist like The Carpenters or Paul McCartney. The bass line from Rhino slowly develops and gets more adventurous as the track goes on – something that would become his signature style with Quo as the years ticked onwards. Despite being a rather positive production in all other areas, the piezo pickups on the electric-acoustic guitars don't just date the record but actively seem to work against it. Had this composition been recorded with standard acoustic guitars and some live strings, it could have been a contender for a single if Quo's audience had the taste for another Rossi ballad.

One of very few outtakes from the sessions was a Williams and Parfitt track called 'Blondes Don't Lie'. A recording is readily available to hear of this song recorded at either Parfitt or William's home studio before departing for the Bahamas, but it exists only in demo form with a lifeless drum machine backing and staccato synth bass. Williams plays some exciting lead guitar in places, but the track was a throwaway idea that would maybe have ended up as B-side material should it have been finished.

Pip Williams posted this on the *SQMB* on 20 September 2008:

> I believe 'Blondes Don't Lie' was one of a whole batch of songs written by Rick and myself in my home studio around '88/'89. It was probably not considered good enough at the time for the *PR* album, but... some might consider it a darn sight better than some of the material that did make it!

Quo only toured the album for 17 dates at the back end of 1989 – supported by Norwegian soft-rock band Evenrude – all of which took place in the UK. The show at Birmingham N.E.C. on 18 December was filmed and subsequently released on VHS as *Rockin' All Over the Years,* with the notable exception of 'Rain' after a camera crane hit the backline and an issue with the stage amplifiers rendered the audio unusable. Rich saved the day by keeping the groove going while the crew swiftly fixed the issue and the band eventually finished the song as normal. By the time Quo toured Europe again for nine dates in the summer of 1990, all of the songs from the album ('Perfect Remedy', 'Little Dreamer' & 'The Power of Rock') had been dropped from the setlist.

While the album's lukewarm reception may not have been the high point the band envisioned for the end to the decade, it served as a steep learning curve for an established band now re-finding its feet after the most turbulent decade in its history. It would also be the last full studio Quo album that Pip Williams would produce until 1996, leaving Rossi to flex his producing muscles again for Quo's next two studio albums. And, while *Perfect Remedy* didn't live up to its name and forged itself a legacy for being the most shunned album this line up of the band would record, it is the perfect snapshot of where all five members were at the time in their personal and creative lives. The only way was up…

Epilogue

The 1980s saw Status Quo endure and overcome more than they would through any other decade. It was even during the *Remedy* sessions that Rossi finally made the decision to stop taking cocaine after simply losing interest. He had given up drugs around the time he settled with his life-partner Eileen Quinn (whom he would later marry in 1991) in early 1989 and after being clean for a short time, decided on one final experiment with cocaine out in Nassau, which finally convinced him that hard drugs were no longer to be a part of his life in or out of Status Quo. Parfitt would also allegedly break his cocaine habit soon after Rossi but found coming off of Rohypnol (sleeping tablets) much harder.

Rick Parfitt said in *Record Collector* in November 2009:

> I really did regret losing so much of the '80s. That was because of drugs and alcohol. I lost so much of it. This is awful, but I don't even remember changing a nappy for my first three kids… I do regret it.

The '80s saw two established members of the band leave, the loss of Heidi Parfitt, and the complete (but temporary) break-up of the band. Failed marriages, failed records and failings in the band's financial management that would take over a decade to resolve also reared their ugly heads.

But 1989 was a year of repair for the band – Rossi and Parfitt were both now in steady, happy relationships; both were getting clean and the band's finances were beginning to show signs of growth thanks to David Walker, who would ultimately keep the Quo brand afloat through the 1990s – what Rhino Edwards would later refer to as the 'lean years'.

Quo would go on to release four studio albums in the '90s, with '91's *Rock til You Drop* peaking at number ten, '94's *Thirsty Work* at number 13, '96's *Don't Stop* at number two and '99's *Under the Influence* at number 26. While the first and last of these were considered a return to form by many, *Don't Stop* would set a precedent for the band recording covers albums – later considered by band and fans alike to be a low point for Status Quo. Although most of the single releases would only just break the UK Top 40, only Quo's 'Anniversary Waltz' (no relation to the 1940s jazz standard by Franklin & Dubin and not in triple time either) could be considered a 'smash' hit single – or pair of singles. Released in two halves in 1990, this medley of covers of old rock 'n' roll standards put Quo back on the map as far as hits were concerned. A single release for 'The Power of Rock' had been planned, but Walker insisted on pulling it, knowing that what Quo needed was a big hit – not another minor hit that would sneak in and out of the chart in a week or two. Inspired by the hits of Jive Bunny, and never one to shy away from a trend, Walker had the band record the medley live at Bray Studios and Rossi and Williams mixed it at Rossi's home studio. Each half peaked at number two and number 16 respectively in the winter of 1990.

David Walker fulfilled his promise to Rossi and Parfitt to fix their extensive money issues, but it came at a detrimental cost to the pair's mental health, and whatever artistic credibility they had with some fans and the serious music critics. Not only was Walker astute enough to negotiate a hefty fee for himself, but he made the band work harder than they ever did to wriggle free from their debts. He was a genius PR man who would see the band play anniversary shows at Butlins Minehead (where the original band cut their teeth as a live act) and attempt to set world records for most shows played in a day to promote the *Rock til You Drop* album – all with extensive television coverage and high profile guests in attendance. They even attempted to sue BBC Radio 1 for not playing their records in a significantly backfiring PR move.

While Status Quo clearly abandoned some of the musical characteristics in the 1980s that made them a household name in the 1970s, it's unfair to expect them to remain musically static as their name would suggest. Artists have to be allowed to grow, develop, and experiment, sometimes even at the expense of critical acclaim or people-pleasing – as difficult as that is to palate for a loyal fanbase. Many creatives in all disciplines are revered for their ability to transform or reinvent themselves several times over. Perhaps it's Quo's name itself that promised the original fans what no artist should be expected to deliver – a lack of progression. Even if the line-up had stayed exactly the same for the band's entire 60-year career, the best gift they could have given their fans would still be the vast choice of what to listen to on any given day. To be able to dip in and out of their varied back-catalogue at will should be any patron's dream. In the immortal words of Andrew Bown; you pay your money, you take your choice.

Status Quo may have become a brand by the 1990s, but it never stopped being a band and one that has sailed quite comfortably into the 21st Century through choppy waters and continues (at the time of writing) to not only make hit records but sell out shows across the world – British institutions indeed.

On Track series

Alan Parsons Project – Steve Swift 978-1-78952-154-2
Tori Amos – Lisa Torem 978-1-78952-142-9
Asia – Peter Braidis 978-1-78952-099-6
Badfinger – Robert Day-Webb 978-1-878952-176-4
Barclay James Harvest – Keith and Monica Domone 978-1-78952-067-5
The Beatles – Andrew Wild 978-1-78952-009-5
The Beatles Solo 1969-1980 – Andrew Wild 978-1-78952-030-9
Blue Oyster Cult – Jacob Holm-Lupo 978-1-78952-007-1
Blur – Matt Bishop – 978-178952-164-1
Marc Bolan and T.Rex – Peter Gallagher 978-1-78952-124-5
Kate Bush – Bill Thomas 978-1-78952-097-2
Camel – Hamish Kuzminski 978-1-78952-040-8
Caravan – Andy Boot 978-1-78952-127-6
Cardiacs – Eric Benac 978-1-78952-131-3
Eric Clapton Solo – Andrew Wild 978-1-78952-141-2
The Clash – Nick Assirati 978-1-78952-077-4
Crosby, Stills and Nash – Andrew Wild 978-1-78952-039-2
The Damned – Morgan Brown 978-1-78952-136-8
Deep Purple and Rainbow 1968-79 – Steve Pilkington 978-1-78952-002-6
Dire Straits – Andrew Wild 978-1-78952-044-6
The Doors – Tony Thompson 978-1-78952-137-5
Dream Theater – Jordan Blum 978-1-78952-050-7
Electric Light Orchestra – Barry Delve 978-1-78952-152-8
Elvis Costello and The Attractions – Georg Purvis 978-1-78952-129-0
Emerson Lake and Palmer – Mike Goode 978-1-78952-000-2
Fairport Convention – Kevan Furbank 978-1-78952-051-4
Peter Gabriel – Graeme Scarfe 978-1-78952-138-2
Genesis – Stuart MacFarlane 978-1-78952-005-7
Gentle Giant – Gary Steel 978-1-78952-058-3
Gong – Kevan Furbank 978-1-78952-082-8
Hall and Oates – Ian Abrahams 978-1-78952-167-2
Hawkwind – Duncan Harris 978-1-78952-052-1
Peter Hammill – Richard Rees Jones 978-1-78952-163-4
Roy Harper – Opher Goodwin 978-1-78952-130-6
Jimi Hendrix – Emma Stott 978-1-78952-175-7
The Hollies – Andrew Darlington 978-1-78952-159-7
Iron Maiden – Steve Pilkington 978-1-78952-061-3
Jefferson Airplane – Richard Butterworth 978-1-78952-143-6
Jethro Tull – Jordan Blum 978-1-78952-016-3
Elton John in the 1970s – Peter Kearns 978-1-78952-034-7
The Incredible String Band – Tim Moon 978-1-78952-107-8
Iron Maiden – Steve Pilkington 978-1-78952-061-3
Judas Priest – John Tucker 978-1-78952-018-7
Kansas – Kevin Cummings 978-1-78952-057-6
The Kinks – Martin Hutchinson 978-1-78952-172-6
Korn – Matt Karpe 978-1-78952-153-5

Led Zeppelin – Steve Pilkington 978-1-78952-151-1
Level 42 – Matt Philips 978-1-78952-102-3
Little Feat – 978-1-78952-168-9
Aimee Mann – Jez Rowden 978-1-78952-036-1
Joni Mitchell – Peter Kearns 978-1-78952-081-1
The Moody Blues – Geoffrey Feakes 978-1-78952-042-2
Motorhead – Duncan Harris 978-1-78952-173-3
Mike Oldfield – Ryan Yard 978-1-78952-060-6
Opeth – Jordan Blum 978-1-78-952-166-5
Tom Petty – Richard James 978-1-78952-128-3
Porcupine Tree – Nick Holmes 978-1-78952-144-3
Queen – Andrew Wild 978-1-78952-003-3
Radiohead – William Allen 978-1-78952-149-8
Renaissance – David Detmer 978-1-78952-062-0
The Rolling Stones 1963-80 – Steve Pilkington 978-1-78952-017-0
The Smiths and Morrissey – Tommy Gunnarsson 978-1-78952-140-5
Status Quo the Frantic Four Years – Richard James 978-1-78952-160-3
Steely Dan – Jez Rowden 978-1-78952-043-9
Steve Hackett – Geoffrey Feakes 978-1-78952-098-9
Thin Lizzy – Graeme Stroud 978-1-78952-064-4
Toto – Jacob Holm-Lupo 978-1-78952-019-4
U2 – Eoghan Lyng 978-1-78952-078-1
UFO – Richard James 978-1-78952-073-6
The Who – Geoffrey Feakes 978-1-78952-076-7
Roy Wood and the Move – James R Turner 978-1-78952-008-8
Van Der Graaf Generator – Dan Coffey 978-1-78952-031-6
Yes – Stephen Lambe 978-1-78952-001-9
Frank Zappa 1966 to 1979 – Eric Benac 978-1-78952-033-0
Warren Zevon – Peter Gallagher 978-1-78952-170-2
10CC – Peter Kearns 978-1-78952-054-5

Decades Series

The Bee Gees in the 1960s – Andrew Mon Hughes et al 978-1-78952-148-1
The Bee Gees in the 1970s – Andrew Mon Hughes et al 978-1-78952-179-5
Black Sabbath in the 1970s – Chris Sutton 978-1-78952-171-9
Britpop – Peter Richard Adams and Matt Pooler 978-1-78952-169-6
Alice Cooper in the 1970s – Chris Sutton 978-1-78952-104-7
Curved Air in the 1970s – Laura Shenton 978-1-78952-069-9
Bob Dylan in the 1980s – Don Klees 978-1-78952-157-3
Fleetwood Mac in the 1970s – Andrew Wild 978-1-78952-105-4
Focus in the 1970s – Stephen Lambe 978-1-78952-079-8
Free and Bad Company in the 1970s – John Van der Kiste 978-1-78952-178-8
Genesis in the 1970s – Bill Thomas 978178952-146-7
George Harrison in the 1970s – Eoghan Lyng 978-1-78952-174-0
Marillion in the 1980s – Nathaniel Webb 978-1-78952-065-1
Mott the Hoople and Ian Hunter in the 1970s – John Van der Kiste
978-1-78-952-162-7
Pink Floyd In The 1970s – Georg Purvis 978-1-78952-072-9

Tangerine Dream in the 1970s – Stephen Palmer 978-1-78952-161-0
The Sweet in the 1970s – Darren Johnson from Gary Cosby collection 978-1-78952-139-9
Uriah Heep in the 1970s – Steve Pilkington 978-1-78952-103-0
Yes in the 1980s – Stephen Lambe with David Watkinson 978-1-78952-125-2

On Screen series
Carry On... – Stephen Lambe 978-1-78952-004-0
David Cronenberg – Patrick Chapman 978-1-78952-071-2
Doctor Who: The David Tennant Years – Jamie Hailstone 978-1-78952-066-8
James Bond – Andrew Wild – 978-1-78952-010-1
Monty Python – Steve Pilkington 978-1-78952-047-7
Seinfeld Seasons 1 to 5 – Stephen Lambe 978-1-78952-012-5

Other Books
1967: A Year In Psychedelic Rock – Kevan Furbank 978-1-78952-155-9
1970: A Year In Rock – John Van der Kiste 978-1-78952-147-4
1973: The Golden Year of Progressive Rock 978-1-78952-165-8
Babysitting A Band On The Rocks – G.D. Praetorius 978-1-78952-106-1
Eric Clapton Sessions – Andrew Wild 978-1-78952-177-1
Derek Taylor: For Your Radioactive Children – Andrew Darlington 978-1-78952-038-5
The Golden Road: The Recording History of The Grateful Dead – John Kilbride 978-1-78952-156-6
Iggy and The Stooges On Stage\' 1967-1974 – Per Nilsen 978-1-78952-101-6
Jon Anderson and the Warriors – the road to Yes – David Watkinson 978-1-78952-059-0
Nu Metal: A Definitive Guide – Matt Karpe 978-1-78952-063-7
Tommy Bolin: In and Out of Deep Purple – Laura Shenton 978-1-78952-070-5
Maximum Darkness – Deke Leonard 978-1-78952-048-4
Maybe I Should've Stayed In Bed – Deke Leonard 978-1-78952-053-8
The Twang Dynasty – Deke Leonard 978-1-78952-049-1

and many more to come!

Would you like to write for Sonicbond Publishing?

At Sonicbond Publishing we are always on the look-out for authors, particularly for our two main series:

On Track. Mixing fact with in depth analysis, the On Track series examines the work of a particular musical artist or group. All genres are considered from easy listening and jazz to 60s soul to 90s pop, via rock and metal.

On Screen. This series looks at the world of film and television. Subjects considered include directors, actors and writers, as well as entire television and film series. As with the On Track series, we balance fact with analysis.

While professional writing experience would, of course, be an advantage the most important qualification is to have real enthusiasm and knowledge of your subject. First-time authors are welcomed, but the ability to write well in English is essential.

Sonicbond Publishing has distribution throughout Europe and North America, and all books are also published in E-book form. Authors will be paid a royalty based on sales of their book.

Further details are available from www.sonicbondpublishing.co.uk. To contact us, complete the contact form there or email info@sonicbondpublishing.co.uk